POTTERYBARN

bedrooms

TEXT
sarah lynch

PHOTOGRAPHY
prue ruscoe

STYLING
edward peterson

EXECUTIVE EDITOR
clay ide

Oxmoor House®

Oxmoor House

Oxmoor House books are distributed by Sunset Books
80 Willow Road, Menlo Park, CA 94025

Oxmoor House and Sunset Books are divisions of
Southern Progress Corporation

SUNSET BOOKS

Vice President, General Manager Rich Smeby
Vice President, Editorial Director Bob Doyle
National Account Manager Brad Moses

POTTERY BARN

President Laura Alber
Senior Vice President, Design & Product Development Celia Tejada
Vice President, Creative Services Clay Ide
Editor Samantha Moss
Photo Coordinator, Special Projects Gina Risso

WELDON OWEN

Chief Executive Officer John Owen
President Terry Newell
Chief Operating Officer Larry Partington
Vice President, International Sales Stuart Laurence

Creative Director Gaye Allen
Vice President, Publisher Roger Shaw
Business Manager Richard Van Oosterhout

Associate Publisher Shawna Mullen
Art Director Colin Wheatland
Managing Editor Peter Cieply
Production Director Chris Hemesath
Color Manager Teri Bell
Photo Coordinator Elizabeth Lazich

Pottery Barn Bedrooms was conceived and produced by
Weldon Owen Inc.
814 Montgomery Street, San Francisco, CA 94133
in collaboration with Pottery Barn
3250 Van Ness Avenue, San Francisco, CA 94109

Set in Simoncini Garamond™ and Formata™

Color separations by AGT–Seattle
Printed in Singapore by Tien Wah Press (Pte.) Ltd.

First printed 2003
10 9 8 7 6 5 4

Library of Congress Control Number 2003106155
ISBN 0-8487-2760-6

The Most Intimate Space

Home is a place of sanctuary, and no room gives us a more profound sense of shelter than the bedroom. It is where we find respite from our daily cares, and an intimate space that clearly expresses our identity. Furnished with individual style, a bedroom can be a comfortable, personal place to rest, relax, read to children, and even work. As the room where we rest and restore, a bedroom must convey warmth and softness, comfort and serenity.

At Pottery Barn, we're devoted to the idea that your home can be an endless source of inspiration. We believe that decorating with style should be easy and fun, and a large part of our mission is to demystify the concept of interior decorating. We design our furnishings to work in many different spaces, and we fill our catalogs with inventive, achievable ideas. This book is full of inspiration and tips we've gleaned from decorating more than five thousand rooms over the past ten years. We shoot all our photography in real homes, often in one day, so our ideas must always be accessible and easy to accomplish. What we've learned over the years is that any bedroom, anywhere, offers unique creative opportunities. We believe your home should be an expression of you, your family, and your lifestyle. In *Pottery Barn Bedrooms*, you'll see how easy it is to create comfortable bedrooms and other sleeping spaces with a sense of style that's all your own.

THE POTTERY BARN DESIGN TEAM

contents

your style

The best bedrooms are inviting, stylish, and full of informal luxury. What's most important in a bedroom is not simply finding a style, but discovering your style. Your bedroom is a place to express your distinct tastes and passion for life. Decorating this space offers the unique opportunity to create a private haven for your enjoyment alone. The trick to finding your own style and creating a perfect bedroom? Start with the basics. Build a solid framework for a room that's soothing and versatile, and then evolve it, customize it, and make it your own.

storage, flexible lighting that allows you to read, relax, or dream, and plenty of pillows. As with any room, well-made furnishings offer the best promise of success. The right foundation pieces not only are timeless, they also give you the freedom to add personal effects or stylish accessories and change the room's style over time. Then, the space can be as pared-down or luxuriously layered as suits you at any given moment.

Think beyond the bedroom, too. Most of us have a few favorite places where we nap or sleep: a plump sofa, an inviting daybed, a sun-filled

A perfect bedroom is both stylishly practical and seductively comfortable. Create a room that's a great canvas for the things that you love.

As we spend more time at home, our bedrooms need to be multifunctional. They're places not only to sleep, but also to dress, have breakfast, relax with family, work, and exercise – in short, rooms where much of a day could easily be spent. Opening up sleeping spaces to other aspects of our lives means adopting a new approach to the use of space and to the way it's styled. Decorating the bedroom has become a balance of crafting a well-functioning space while preserving a sense of intimacy and serenity.

A comfortable bed is the first essential. Find a style that's just right, whether for lounging or working on a laptop. Add abundant (or clever)

window seat, or a cool hammock. Each deserves special attention and should be styled to create a restorative space. A guest bedroom also requires careful thought, especially if you use it as an office or study when company's not around.

The sleeping spaces in these pages offer ideas to help you create your own sanctuary and define your own style. From textures that place warmth and comfort where it's most needed to color palettes, furnishings, accessories, and display ideas, you'll see a wealth of options to help you decide what's right for you. Inspired by these ideas, you can easily create a warm and inviting bedroom that expresses your personal style.

The Basics of Bedroom Style

When you're planning the perfect bedroom, no detail is small: fresh linens, textures that envelop you with warmth and luxury, adjustable lighting at your fingertips, comfortable furnishings. The rule here is simple: if it makes you comfortable, it works.

Whether you're planning simply to add new accessories to your bedroom or to redecorate completely, choose furnishings and details that reward you with delight. For some, the ideal is a room with lots of accessories and places for display. For others, a simple and streamlined design establishes the perfect atmosphere for relaxation. Whichever approach is right for you, begin with a strong foundation – shapely furnishings, a palette based in flexible neutrals, and good lighting. This cottage bedroom is a perfect example. Though the room is not enormous, its simple design contains everything an ideal bedroom should have, in an easy combination of comfort and style.

Furnishings are eclectic and convey a sophisticated but casual sensibility, and the design pays attention to practical matters. The arrangement is welcoming and easy to navigate, and furniture is suited to more than one function. The room has places to relax, to work, and to read, as well as ample storage for belongings. The bed is well stocked with soft pillows, blankets, and throws that can be used or turned back as temperature and comfort require.

Tiers of texture, *left*, on a bed invite long mornings curled up under the covers. The white cotton bed skirt and hemstitched sheets are topped with a hemstitched duvet and shams, plenty of pillows, and layers of throws: faux fur, fringed white wool, and gray flannel. **A pair of branches**, *right*, used as curtain rods, give a casual lift to pooled linen curtains. They hang from looped rawhide ties that are simply tacked to the door frame.

Most bedrooms feel more welcoming when they have zones carved out for the pursuit of leisure, whether for enjoying morning coffee or reading a good book. Here, two leather club chairs are pulled up to the fireplace and topped with lambswool throws for even greater comfort. Layered rugs – looped wool over jute – define the bed and reading areas. Pine-plank flooring surrounds this soft island of texture. As in the rest of the house, no luxury in the bedroom is more coveted than a steady stream of daylight. Where space permits, cluster chairs or chaises by a window to take full advantage of the sun.

A fieldstone fireplace is a dramatic focal point. It's a logical choice to position a bed facing such a grand fixture. In winter, the flickering flames are visible from every part of the room. When warm weather arrives, turn the hearth into an indoor garden by filling it with fresh plants, flowers, or bundles of gathered twigs. Or, change the scene with a decorative screen that can be moved aside when the fireplace is in use.

Lambswool throws, *left*, add irresistible warmth and comfort; hand-carved accessories add texture. **A mantel is a natural showcase**, *right*, for artwork and displays, allowing walls to remain clutter-free and enhancing the sense of space. A moss-covered tree branch displays Victorian beaded flowers, old photos, and other mementos.

Clever, organized storage is a key ingredient for any comfortable bedroom, particularly if a room lacks closet space or a separate dressing area. If your room has only one closet, look elsewhere for inventive storage solutions. Fill under-bed and under-table space with handsome baskets and containers for keeping everyday items close at hand.

Even the tiniest space offers possibilities for clever storage. Look for decorative and inventive solutions that blend into a room's decor.

Maximize the use of vertical space with hanging shelves, and use hooks to store linens, towels, robes, and clothing. Here, a ladder in the bath holds towels, and a ladder-back chair, placed strategically between the dressing area and bathroom, offers both seating and storage. Items can be tucked into a basket underneath the chair, and clothing or towels can be hung or draped over its back.

A small bathroom, *left*, uses limited space to its fullest; a ladder and basket hold towels and reinforce the rustic country feel. **This tiny but well-planned closet**, *right*, is outfitted with a step stool and built-in and hanging shelves. The mirror on the plank door stands in for a vanity.

Design Details

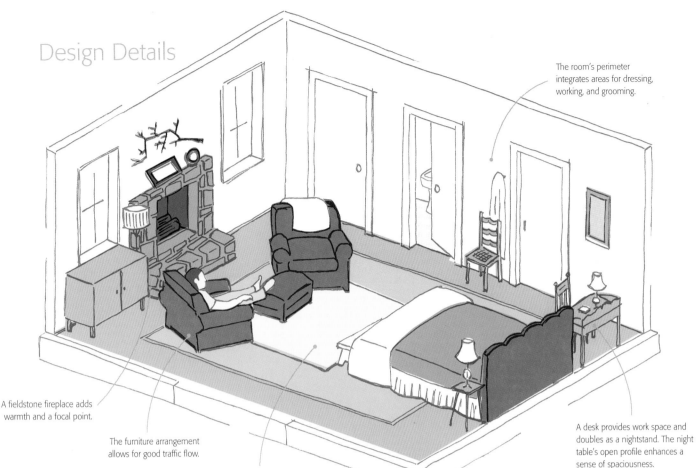

The room's perimeter integrates areas for dressing, working, and grooming.

A fieldstone fireplace adds warmth and a focal point.

The furniture arrangement allows for good traffic flow.

Layered rugs help define a cozy conversation area.

A desk provides work space and doubles as a nightstand. The night table's open profile enhances a sense of spaciousness.

Color Palette

Neutrals are always good choices for bedrooms because they create an atmosphere of calm. In the absence of bold color, the mind can let go of any pre-conceived color associations and be at peace. Use natural materials like leather, wood, and stone to strengthen a neutral palette. Here, quiet shades, such as the deep chocolate brown of tanned leather and the lighter amber hue of pine-plank flooring, create a homey feeling.

Room Plan

This bedroom carves out specialized areas for sleeping, working, dressing, relaxing, and conversing, without making the room feel compartmentalized. The layered rugs create a central space for the main elements: the bed and the hearthside conversation area. The soft, looped-wool rug, from the foot of the bed to the club chairs, adds luxury to this core of activity. Areas for working, dressing, and grooming mark the perimeter while still feeling like part of the whole space. A desk at one side of the bed doubles as a nightstand and a home-office space.

Materials

Jute Soft and durable, rugs woven of this strong plant fiber are perfect for high-traffic areas.

Fieldstone A classic fireplace of rough fieldstone has a rustic, hand-hewn quality. Quarry-cut stone, in contrast, is smoother and more regularly shaped.

Leather The dimensions, surface texture, softness, and pigment regularity of the hide all distinguish high-quality leather.

space

Space is the blank canvas you get to work with when you move into a new home. An empty room can be as challenging to a homeowner as a blank page is to a writer – and just as satisfying once you've figured out what you want to say. If you're designing your dream home, you may have the luxury of deciding how many square feet will go where. But most of us work within existing rooms, squeeze favorite possessions into new spaces, and see the spaces transformed. The size of a room may determine proportion, but it needn't limit your imagination.

Making a success of a small space remains the greatest challenge for many of us, but the imagination and ingenuity required often result in unexpected charm. Every part of the room offers storage possibilities – overhead and under furniture, on floors and on walls. Look for items that can be hung, tucked beneath the bed, or stored up high out of sight. Dual-purpose furniture like daybeds and nesting tables also help make economic use of limited space, while floating shelves (rather than solid bookcases) and hanging lights (instead of standing lamps) expand visual space.

Space is both physical and sensory. It's the footprint of a room; it's also a feeling. In bedrooms, the use of space should create a sense of warmth.

The placement of furniture dictates a bedroom's flow of traffic and defines sleeping, dressing, and conversation areas. It helps determine whether the room has a snug, secluded feel or an open, airy one. Warm colors, plush textures, and casual clutter make a room seem more intimate, while pale colors, sleek surfaces, and minimal styling make even the smallest room seem spacious.

Lighting has a powerful effect on our perception of space. Fluorescent bulbs cast a cool and contemporary light; incandescent lamps give off a warm glow. Bright light, especially natural light, makes a room seem more open, while candlelight creates a sense of intimacy and drama.

Large bedrooms demand a different approach, especially if your aspirations include a sense of intimacy. Start by delineating discrete areas with an arrangement of sofas, chaise longues, or easy chairs. Define a reading nook or dressing space with an area rug in a rich tone. Pull your bed out from the wall, and drape it in layers of fabric.

Whatever the size of your bedroom, little touches count for a lot. Flowers on the night table scent the air. A plush rug eases the cold on winter nights. A chenille throw folded at the foot of the bed invites an afternoon nap. It's not a showcase you're creating, but a personal haven. Make it inviting, make it soothing, make it yours.

A Backyard Bedroom

Create extra space with a fanciful take on a guest house. This outdoor bedroom optimizes one-room living with space-saving solutions, abundant light, and well-planned storage. With room enough for a bed, desk, and dressing area, the confines of a tent never seemed so sumptuous.

Architectural wisdom says that a good design must be well built and useful – and offer a large measure of delight. This tiny warm-weather bedroom, built as a permanent tent with removable canvas walls, incorporates much to delight in, with all the comforts of its indoor equivalent. Despite its small size, the room conveys a remarkable sense of spaciousness, thanks to its use of efficient organization, small-scale furnishings, and whimsical decor.

To make any room appear larger than it really is, the first trick is to use effective lighting and a pale, subtly varied color palette. Fitted with glass windows and a French door, this tent also receives plenty of illumination through its fabric walls, which fill the space with light during the day. Although fabric isn't generally an option for indoor walls, you could achieve a similar effect with pure white walls and sheer curtains or linen shades in any room with good sun exposure. The daytime effect of light filtered through canvas walls repeats at night, when lamplight filters gently through the canopy of mosquito netting hung above an iron bed. A kerosene lantern, hung outside from the eaves, lights the entry and serves as a welcoming beacon to visitors.

Quilts are the perfect small-room accessory, *left*. Offering layers of warmth and bringing color and pattern to the room, they're a cheerful reminder of country style. **Extend a small space**, *right*, by annexing an entryway. This deck is treated like a room in itself, with chairs and pillows set up for lounging.

Designed with an eye
for detail, a unique guest
tent can be a space for
comfort and relaxation.

In a small space, the right plan can
artfully incorporate more furnishings
than you might expect. Stacked white
storage cubes draw attention upward
and make an under-eave space appear
taller, while providing ample room
to store clothing. Camp furnishings,
such as folding tables and chairs, are
flexible and have a slimmer profile
than indoor items. A secretary serves
as both desk and nightstand, and
closes to hide clutter. A restored
steamer trunk offers seating and
storage. Anything that can serve
more than one purpose is especially
welcome in a small space.

Much of this room's special appeal
derives from its surprising structure,
but you could easily replicate its
visual punch in an attic room or loft.
Take it literally (see Room Resources,
page 182, for information on
purchasing these tents), or adapt
the idea to suit your own setup.

Decorated for comfort, *left*, this guest tent
offers lots of amenities: electricity, plenty of space
for books, and room for a display of vintage glass
bottles. A painted wooden sign is fitted with
hooks for hats. **A netting canopy**, *right*, creates an
intimate, light-filtering enclosure over an iron bed.

Where space is limited, it might seem like accessories would be, too, but this is not necessarily the case. If you look carefully, you'll find plenty of corners in which to tuck favorite finds. In fact, the small size of a room draws more attention to collectibles, especially if you use them daily. Mirrors are a wonderful example. Choose a vintage pair and use them to flank a door in a small bedroom. They visually expand the space and become a key part of the decor at the same time.

Small spaces need careful planning. Use furnishings and accents that are both functional and beautiful.

Even when necessities take up all the available surface areas in a small bedroom, there's no reason the necessities can't also be fun. In this room, a rough-hewn Adirondack table and stool accessorized with a wooden treen mirror create a compact vanity. A vintage hairbrush set and luxurious toiletries play against the room's more utilitarian design elements.

A window shade, *left*, is cleverly fashioned from a painter's canvas drop cloth with rawhide lacing and grommets set in binding tape trim. **A mottled 1950s-style mirror**, *right*, subtly reflects light. The fishing creel tucked under the window plays up the rustic look and makes a great storage basket.

Design Details

Color Palette

The spirit of this outdoor bedroom harks back to childhood summer camp. A pure and natural color palette reinforces the atmosphere of a relaxed getaway. The removable canvas walls and sheer fabric curtains are a natural off-white that turns a warmer shade when illuminated with the light of dawn or early dusk. A blue-gray, white-edged floor grounds the structure with a sense of permanence. The tent's honey-colored wood frame harmonizes with wood furniture and brightly colored accents.

Materials

Canvas In all its waterproof and durable glory, canvas is a sure sign of warm-weather activity. Commonly used for manufacturing sporting goods, awnings, and outdoor furnishings, this heavy-duty cotton material connotes fun and relaxation.

Sheer cotton Sheer, lightweight cotton is reminiscent of warm climates. In pure white, this natural fabric reveals its weave when hung as a breezy drape or room screen, permitting light to shine through. Linen offers a similar look.

Quilt A colorful patchwork quilt gives a room an instant sense of tradition and homeyness. Patchwork may have been born of a necessity to recycle scraps of fabric, but sewing together different fabrics soon became an American art form and a traditional gift of love and remembrance.

Every item in a small space must work hard to make the most of the floor plan and to add to the overall sense of space. The simple painted gray floor here is left unadorned, with a narrow band of white offering the barest definition of a summer "rug." Connecting indoors with outdoors works especially well to expand small spaces, whether through a window, porch, or entryway. Borrowing space from the outside can make a small space feel larger and more gracious. Take an informal approach inside and out, with casual pieces that set the tone before you enter.

Palm fronds, *left*, form a leggy entryway table, and an antique wrought-iron mirror by the French door creates a faux window.
A colorful folding chair and lantern, *above*, line up on the front porch and invite company to come calling.

Creating a Siesta Space

Who says sleeping spaces have to be kept indoors? Stake out a shaded corner of a porch, deck, or veranda and create a fresh-air alcove for leisurely afternoon napping and relaxing.

Savor summer by extending your living space outside during the warm months. This shady porch was transformed into a napping area by bringing in a hammock, a bright woven rug, cotton plaids and stripes, and a breezy linen window shade.

Following the lead of its indoor counterparts, this open-air room is comfortably outfitted with ample pillows and plump seat cushions, as well as furnishings that can withstand the elements. Your own siesta space doesn't have to be large (even a corner of a patio will do), but it should always be soothing and peaceful.

This window seat, *left*, doubles as an alfresco dining nook for casual meals and card games. **A roomy hammock**, *right*, is one of life's greatest pleasures, the perfect spot to embrace the breezes on a summer afternoon.

A Family-Friendly Bedroom

The new spacious master bedroom is a casual spot where kids play while Mom and Dad relax. Soft, low-maintenance furnishings create a space that's as welcoming to children as it is to adults. By making the room accessible to everyone, you can spend more time together as a family.

For a large number of families, the master bedroom already functions as a sort of informal second living room – a place to hang out, watch TV, read, relax, and reconnect. With well-chosen furnishings, you can turn the inevitable into the enviable: a snug haven that's safe for kids, low-maintenance for parents, attractively designed, and welcoming to all.

Every element of this bedroom takes into account child accessibility and safety. A step stool helps toddlers climb onto the bed for reading, napping, or watching movies. Dressed with several layers of bedding, including a highly durable denim duvet cover, the bed can easily lose a layer to the wash and still look finished and inviting.

Using white furnishings, bedding, and slipcovers and pickled pine-plank flooring may seem like a risky choice with children around. In fact, white is the easiest color to get clean. While colors and patterns can fade and grow dull from repeated washings, white fabric can be bleached and hung to dry in the sun. Denim is another kid-friendly fabric because it fades beautifully and gets softer with washing.

A step stool up to the bed, *left*, and other thoughtful additions like soft upholstered cubes, offer kids the same access to the room as adults. The children's portraits hang over the bed. **Turn pieces of a favorite baby quilt**, *right*, into pillows or wall hangings to bring a personal touch to the room. Fabric need not be discarded just because it's old or worn.

Paired with kid-friendly furniture, washable fabrics make it easy to transform a bedroom into a communal family space. The area in front of a gas-burning fireplace is designed as a place where kids can play, read, or work on projects. A soft wool rug, slipcovered chaise, and child-sized chairs carve out an inviting seating area where children

A family bedroom embraces the best of two worlds: play area and soothing retreat.

can cuddle with parents in front of a fire. Built-in cupboards and recessed bookshelves provide clutter-resistant storage while framing the stone fireplace within their crisp lines. An easy-to-clean floor of pickled pine boards with a semigloss topcoat takes the worry out of spills and art projects. A soothing palette of pale green and white promises to calm energetic toddlers as they settle down for a nap or bedtime story.

Mom and Dad's personal effects, *left*, are stored out of reach in an alcove between two closets. With no breakable accessories or precariously placed decorations, this room is kid-safe and play-friendly. **The play area**, *right*, easily converts to an inviting parents' corner, with pillows and reading material close at hand.

Keep clutter to a minimum by using a storage ladder to contain toys and projects. Semigloss finishes and washable slipcovers are sensible choices in a family-friendly bedroom.

Design Details

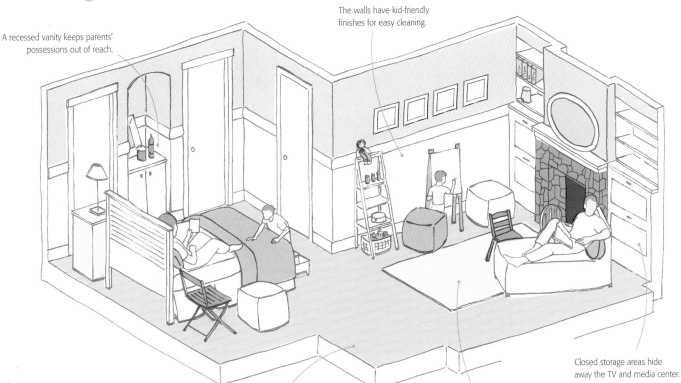

A recessed vanity keeps parents' possessions out of reach.

The walls have kid-friendly finishes for easy cleaning.

Closed storage areas hide away the TV and media center.

Hardwood floors stand up to a family bedroom's heavy traffic.

The rug in front of the fireplace welcomes kids and adults with a soft surface for playing and relaxing.

Color Palette

Celadon, a tint of gray-green or very pale green, is used on the upper walls to create a calm backdrop for this family-friendly bedroom. White furnishings, trim, bedding, and pickled plank floors provide soothing accents. From the layered bedding to the slipcovered chaise longue, fabrics in muted yet powerful colors suggest comfort. A blue denim duvet beckons adults and children alike with its homey, familiar feeling.

Room Plan

This L-shaped room was built with zones for the whole family. The fireplace area offers children a soft rug, practical storage, and small-size furnishings. The adult-sized chaise is set at an angle that visually delineates the zones for children from those for adults. The sleeping space is designed for adults but welcoming to kids. A step stool helps little legs climb up, and soft fabric cubes prevent bumps and bruises. Built-in storage spaces, such as an alcove on the far side of the room, recede from view, storing Mom and Dad's things out of sight and children's reach.

Materials

Denim Originally thought to be from France, this durable cotton fabric became popular in America during the California Gold Rush, in the form of work pants (jeans).

Chenille Chenille fabric is woven in tufted cords to create a plush texture that's as durable as it is comfortable.

Twill This strong textile is woven, usually of cotton, to create diagonal ridges across the surface for durability. Denim and gabardine are examples of twill weaves.

How to Make the Most of Space

A cohesive space is always an inviting retreat. Employ the basics of space planning to make the most of what you have. Use color to emphasize or create the illusion of expansiveness by wrapping the room in a single pale hue. Visually extend a wall using the strong horizontal line of a built-in shelf. Use bold patterns to focus attention on an area. When it comes to furniture, keep in mind that you can increase the sense of spaciousness by choosing closed, streamlined storage. Tables, beds, and chairs that sit high off the floor make rooms appear airier and less cluttered.

A small occasional table, *above*, can serve as a vanity in a smaller room. Antiques like this often have slimmer lines and a slightly smaller scale than modern pieces. Use a narrow rectangular mirror to add light and dimension and to lift attention upward, creating the impression of open space. As a rule, furniture shorter than three feet, like this adjustable stool, doesn't intrude into the horizon line of a room, so it appears to take up less space.
A cushioned window seat, *right*, offers a cozy private refuge. Easy to construct, window seats make great use of corner nooks and crannies.

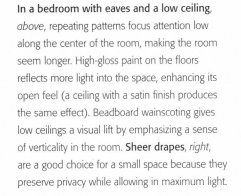

In a bedroom with eaves and a low ceiling, *above*, repeating patterns focus attention low along the center of the room, making the room seem longer. High-gloss paint on the floors reflects more light into the space, enhancing its open feel (a ceiling with a satin finish produces the same effect). Beadboard wainscoting gives low ceilings a visual lift by emphasizing a sense of verticality in the room. **Sheer drapes**, *right*, are a good choice for a small space because they preserve privacy while allowing in maximum light.

color

You've probably heard lots of advice on the importance of color – its psychological effect on a room, the way it draws the eye, and how light colors make a space seem larger. While all of this is helpful, it's often difficult to translate when it comes to decorating your own home. If you're like most people, choosing a color palette comes down to selecting a few hues that you consistently love and some accent colors that complement them. One good way to do this is to use a neutral base palette and bring color into the room through accessories.

Keep in mind how the color makes you feel, and be sure it suits the room's function. If blue gives you the blues, it doesn't matter that it's a "good" color for a bedroom. There's a wealth of information available about the effects of color: red makes us feel energized, blue makes a room seem cooler, pastels are quieting, and deep purples evoke creativity. But the trick is to focus on your own reaction to color. Does it appear calming? Sensual? Clean and fresh, or spicy and exotic? You can give a bedroom these attributes simply by using a color that evokes these feelings.

In a space that greets you every day and sends you off to sleep every night, the colors you choose should feel personal and special – straight from the heart.

To gain confidence with color, use some simple design tricks. First of all, start slowly; bringing a new color scheme into your home is something that takes getting used to. Introduce small doses of a hue you like, in accessories such as a lamp or a vase. If you're happy with the hue, gradually incorporate larger expanses of the color into the room's decor: use it in bedding or slipcovers, or paint an old dresser or wooden chair. If you're feeling daring, go straight for the walls – or paint just one wall. Featuring color on one wall can have a significant impact. Fortunately, paint is relatively inexpensive, so the consequences of changing your mind aren't too great.

Perhaps you are drawn to vibrant shades of ochre and crimson in the fall and hues of green and pink in the spring. Choose a color scheme that accommodates your changing preferences. If you establish a neutral background, you can accent it with bedding, drapes, area rugs, and other accents of color. In this way, you can easily transform the feel of your bedroom from an autumnal enclave to a cheery summer space.

Also, take a cue from what's inside your closet. Hues that you instinctively gravitate toward tend to make you look and feel your best. The same colors that work well in your wardrobe can often work wonders for you in your home.

Red attracts attention, *this page*: scarlet accents give a cottage bedroom a bold update and make it stylish. **A vintage tole table lamp**, *opposite top*, has a striking effect as part of a bold red suite of accessories. **A simple crackle-glazed chest**, *opposite left*, is a graphic block of color against the pristine white background.

Accents of Color

Vividly colored accessories give an all-white bedroom fresh appeal. Brilliant red against bright white creates crisp contrast. Even in small doses, bright color can make a big impact.

Adding color to an all-white room is as simple as painting on a blank canvas. By gradually layering elements onto a neutral background, with a single color or a palette of hues, you can see how much color is just enough. Begin with bed linens or small accessories that can be easily changed. Once you have a palette that pleases you, continue to add increasingly larger doses of color a bit at a time: on mouldings, a chest of drawers, or the inside of a closet door.

Choose shades that are in harmony with the tint of white in the room. Bright white is best offset by cool blues and greens, or by very saturated colors. Ivory goes beautifully with warm tones such as amber or ochre.

A Serene Sanctuary

Restful shades of ocean blues and sea greens call to mind peaceful afternoons at the shore and turn a simple country bedroom into a tranquil retreat. Capture the spirit of water and sky with an aqueous palette that subtly shifts with the day's changing light.

The colors you choose for a room immediately establish its mood. In a bedroom, color – especially on the walls – can mean the difference between creating a tranquil sleeping space, a romantic boudoir, or a vibrant morning room.

When selecting colors for a bedroom, don't worry about rules. Each of us has an innate sense of color, rooted in personal history and geography. Trust your instincts.

While a single color palette employed throughout the house can give it overall harmony, the hues you choose for the bedroom don't need to be perfectly matched to be complementary. Nor do they have to be the colors you're "supposed" to use for bedrooms or with certain architecture or furniture. A neoclassical bedroom suite can be accented with bright fuchsia. A contemporary set can look crisp against restrained, classic colors. A country cottage bedroom can splash out in a modern palette of blues.

Blue is the color most often associated with tranquility and serenity, desirable attributes in a sleeping space. Begin building your palette with the palest blue that appeals to you and use that color for your walls. This gives you the freedom to use deeper hues as accents.

Blue is one of the most popular colors for bedrooms. A single hue might have felt too strong in this low-ceilinged room, but layering blues, whites, and greens throughout lends a comfortable sophistication. **A collection of old bottles,** *right*, adds interest without detracting from the sense of serenity.

Layering different shades of a single palette creates a multifaceted and engaging color design. Tones of blue, green, and lavender can be easily combined if they have a predominantly blue base in common. The same goes for citrus hues: lemon, tangerine, and lime green all blend well if based in yellow. Any combination of shades with a similar base tone can create a pleasing colorscape.

In its daily advance from dawn to dusk, a shifting play of sunlight enlivens blue's subtle character.

Like human moods, colors change throughout the day and are more interesting when they register subtle variations. Combining true blue with lavenders and green-tinged blues creates dimension and presents a palette reminiscent of sea and sky. Light, both natural and artificial, plays an especially important role, transforming a room as it changes from morning through night. Early light is clearer and brings out the crispness of blue. Late light is warmer and emphasizes depth.

With its iron bed, blue stitched quilt, light blue chambray sheets, and silk channel-stitched shams, this cottage bedroom has a clean country style. The turned-leg nightstands, white wainscot trunk, and pickled pine floor enhance the effect.

Design Details

Color Palette

The combination of pale blue walls and light blue, cobalt, and sea green bedding in this bedroom suggests coastal motifs. Paler blue-greens call to mind seaside lounging and tropical beaches. Primary blue, particularly when paired with fresh white, is reminiscent of Mediterranean vistas and nautical adventures. Layering blues, whites, and greens also lends a comfortable sophistication. When mixed with the sandy tones of natural flooring and clean white wainscoting, the watery blues create a soothing place to relax.

Materials

Wainscoting Originally developed to prevent wall damage in heavy-traffic areas, wainscoting usually refers to wooden boards or panels that cover the lower portion of a wall. The term can also refer to full-height wall paneling. Beadboard, which has a regular raised pattern on the wood, is the most common type of wainscoting.

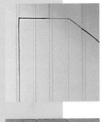

Pickled wood The decorative technique called pickling describes a whitewashing effect that makes pine and other woods look pale and bleached with age.

Quilt The top of a patchwork quilt can be sewn from scraps of fabric or from blocks of fabrics selected for their complementary colors or graphic pattern, such as gingham and plaid. Unlike patchwork, the top of a whole-cloth quilt is a solid piece of fabric, which shows off intricate stitchery.

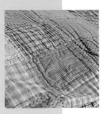

Brave Color

Color is sometimes the best furnishing of all. It can be used to subdue or boldly highlight areas, and it needn't be pale to feel restful. Strong color choices can have surprising effects.

Conventional wisdom has it that blues, greens, and violets are calming, while bright colors are energetic and stimulating. But bedrooms don't have to be painted in soft colors to feel relaxing. An unexpected color choice adds interest to a space and turns color theory on its head.

While you can add color to the bedroom in many ways – through accessories, bedding, or just a few pillows – don't underestimate the power of painting a focal wall. A brave color on a single wall can transform everything around it. Especially in modern spaces, a subtle palette can seem too weak. Vivid colors add life and stand up to strong design.

A boldly painted red wall, *this page*, makes this napping area inviting, especially when combined with accessories in coordinating hues. **An ivory shag rug**, *opposite top*, and white candles in the fireplace temper the bold color of the focal wall. **A rattan trunk**, *opposite right*, holds stacks of blankets coordinated to the palette.

A pale wall color and bedding in
shades of white, *this page,* tone down
the warmth in this bedroom. The mix of
simple cotton and rich silk and chenille
bedding complement each other.

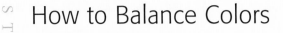

How to Balance Colors

You can change the atmosphere in a room with color alone. It has a powerful effect on our moods. Warm colors (reds, yellows, and oranges) suggest passion and energy. Cool hues (blues, violets, and greens) encourage a mood of peace and calm. Different combinations of bed linens and wall colors can warm up or cool down the total effect, so try adding and subtracting color until the balance feels right to you.

Deep-hued bedding, *left,* envelops a sleeping space in warmth and luxury. Bedding fabrics that reflect light, such as silk and chenille, make colors appear more saturated. **Snowy white linens mixed with icy blue,** *below left,* instantly freshen up a room's cool color palette. **The indigo blue of a denim duvet,** *below,* is calming and soft. Layer the bed with a full spectrum of blues, from pale to dark, for an intensified effect that is still relaxing.

How to Create Mood with Color

Give your bedroom a fresh point of view with a dash of brilliant color. Paint a focal wall, or add personality and warmth simply by bringing in colorful bedding, pillows, throws, or painted furniture. Color offers the ultimate in decorating flexibility. A change of hue can take a room from serene to bold. Use the language of color to evoke feelings: tranquility (blue), inspiration (green), passion (red or pink), or energy (yellow). Begin slowly by dressing the bed with small doses of colorful pillows or a single brilliant throw. When coloring a room, use hues in a range of tones to give texture to the palette.

A hint of pink on turquoise paisley, *opposite top*, suggests the freshness of spring. **A bold splash of ocean blue**, *opposite bottom and center*, on painted shelves and bedding keeps the mood lively but soothing. **Blanket a bed in romance**, *left*, with layers of soft pink and coral against tan and white. **Vivid color combinations**, *below left*, can be chic and sophisticated. **Flowers and botanicals**, *below*, are an easy and fragrant way to add a splash of color to a space. Here, a vibrant pink camellia energizes an Asian-inspired bedside still life.

Warm wall colors

Here, we've chosen a sampling of warm wall colors well suited to the bedroom. Colors like cardinal red, cinnabar, bittersweet orange, and even brighter shades of marigold and amber yellow can instantly make a bedroom feel cozy. Flattering shades of rosy pink and peach tend to create a soothing environment that's ideal for the relaxed space of a bedroom. Especially in climates with long winters, a warm color palette makes getting in and out of bed more inviting.

Neutral wall colors

Many people find that neutral wall colors make a bedroom feel peaceful. Among the many neutrals to choose from are straws, beiges, whites, taupes, and grays. These work in natural combinations to create a tranquil space that easily accommodates a whole range of accent colors.

Cool wall colors

Our sampling of cool colors for bedroom walls includes shades of blues, greens, and teals. These hues take their inspiration from the fresh colors of nature – the sea, the trees, the sky. When used in the bedroom, cool tones impart a sense of expansive openness. According to color theory, blues and blue-greens also tend to have a calming effect. In a warm climate, these colors can make a room feel infinitely soothing – and they can even make it seem a few degrees cooler.

wall, furnishing, and accent colors for your bedroom

How to coordinate colors

We've created this guide to help you choose colors for furnishings and accessories. By using core or basic colors for foundation pieces and layering in coordinating accessories in basic or accent hues, you can easily create a sophisticated palette in your bedroom.

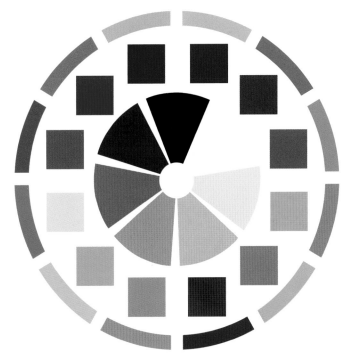

Core colors, shown in the middle, are neutrals that work well as a room's color foundation. Use a monochromatic palette of almond and oat for a tranquil effect, or in combination with accents of white and black for a contemporary look. Core colors are timeless, classic choices for key pieces and larger bedroom furnishings.

Basic colors, shown in the second ring, can work both as foundation and accent tones. This sampling presents a group of hues well-suited to bedroom decor, especially in classic combinations with core colors – lake blue with clean white, cranberry with creamy white, rich wine or sage green with almond.

Accent colors, in the outer ring, add splashes of lively interest to a bedroom. Small details in these fashion colors can be swapped out seasonally. Place hot pink flowers on a night table or a vibrant orange throw on the bed for eye-catching punch. If you're especially bold, you can use these stronger colors for your main palette.

texture

The most subtle and sophisticated way to add interest to any room is to use an assortment of textures and materials. Color can create atmosphere, furnishings may give a room its look, but a mix of textures gives a space soul. For bedrooms, where the sense of touch reigns supreme, texture is truly essential.

Everyone wants a bed that's comfortable and inviting, with blankets and linens that indulge the senses. But texture is important at every level in this room, where your body comes in contact with so many fabrics and finishes. Bedroom

Tactile contrasts increase visual interest. Offset man-made materials with natural ones, smooth surfaces with distressed ones, plush pile carpets with flat-weave rugs. Texture can highlight actual or psychological temperature contrasts as well. Wood floors and leather upholstery near a stone fireplace effect a subtle balance of warm and cool. A modern bedroom feels homier stocked with plump pillows and hand-knit wool throws.

Fabric options are almost limitless, from the gentle weight of well-washed cotton, crisp linen, and cool silk to the comforting warmth of

It's the soft textures in a bedroom that make you want to curl up and linger. Pillows, throws, blankets, shams, and duvets promise warmth and comfort.

floors feel more luxurious when they're warm and cozy underfoot. Surface materials are more enticing when their tactile quality is highlighted.

Texture can be visual, physical, or both. Visual textures play with the light, catching or absorbing it in ways that engage the eye. For example, stripes and other patterns give a sense of texture even to flat objects. Strong texture has the effect of making objects appear heavier; smooth objects appear less weighty. Texture can be used to alter the lines of furniture. Dress a bed with fitted bedding instead of a duvet or bedspread to give it a more tailored profile, or drape a nightstand with a runner to soften its hard edges.

chenille and faux fur. Linen and cotton are time-less, affordable core basics that offer a neutral backdrop for layering. Combine heavier, more luxurious fabrics like cashmere and velvet for a sense of richness, or pair them with simple white cotton to bring a note of texture to an otherwise smooth bed. The real beauty of textured fabrics, however, is in the wide-ranging freedom they offer to mix and match linens and accents without regard to source – old with new, fitted with loose, wool with silk, satin with cotton. Whether you aim for a cool or warm effect, softness is paramount in a bedroom, so treat yourself well with textiles. This is the place to splurge.

Getting White Right

Texture is key in an all-white room. The secret to a successful monochromatic space is combining materials and textures to highlight the subtle beauty of simple things. Softly colored accents add a personal touch without distracting from the serenity of the setting.

Rich, inviting texture – and lots of it – is invaluable when you choose a monochromatic palette. Especially in all-white rooms, where the atmosphere changes with the light, texture adds depth and warmth to every surface.

Like all colors, white has endless tones, from rosy to cool blue or gray tints, and some pairings look better than others. A warm white can make ivory look clean, and a bright white can make blue-white appear calm. If the hues and materials you choose come from a single point of inspiration – for example, beach-toned naturals or winter whites with their icy tints of blue – the combination is known as a chromatic palette. In other words, all the colors will have a similar underlying hue, and they'll make a good match.

This bedroom was painted in a palette of natural tones (sun-bleached white, sand, and honey) to complement its light-filled architecture. White is sometimes considered the hue that people turn to when they're afraid of color, but the truth is that white, when used with courage, can be the most powerful and effective "color" of all.

Texturize all-white beds, *left*, with layers of varied fabric – matelassé, faux fur, chunky woven cotton, and crisp cotton sheeting. Pile on oversized pillows, shams, and throws to create a cozy destination for relaxed Sunday mornings. **A simple shelf**, *right*, does double duty as a nightstand and display area for favorite treasures. The hard textures nicely contrast with the soft bed.

White can give rooms a wonderful atmosphere of extended space and openness. In any bedroom, expansiveness appears best when warmed up with natural materials.

Although more subtle, contrasts in texture can be as effective as those in color. Here, the jacquard coir rug, clean muslin-wrapped headboard, and soft faux-fur throw all contribute visual interest, especially when placed beside the stronger textures of the distressed white lanterns and the whitewashed wallboards. Smooth surfaces can also contribute tactile interest. The golden pine-plank floorboards, chrome floor lamp, and Biedermeier-style table in front of the hearth create an appealing blend of matte and polished.

Shifting light alters the perceived color of white rooms, through the day and season by season. Play up the light in your bedroom with a few well-placed mantel accessories – mercury glass vases, silver frames, sparkling candlesticks, or brushed aluminum accents. They introduce a lustrous element to the room's textures, reflecting glints of illumination.

Raw silk and natural linen, *left,* are hung in place of artwork to create a distinctive focal point that's as quiet and understated as the room. **Add layers of texture,** *right:* mohair and cotton throws and a faux-fur pillow make tailored chairs and a window seat inviting places to rest.

The most comfortable bedrooms evoke a soothing atmosphere where you can retreat from the world. The greatest luxury such rooms afford is a multitude of places to curl up and relax: an oversized bed layered with soft throws, an upholstered easy chair, and a cozy window nook.

Wrap your bedroom in the subtle beauty of texture: the level sheen of polished wood, a light touch of linen, plush cushions, and shapely scrolled seashells.

In this bedroom, a fireside sitting area at the foot of the bed incorporates variations on a natural theme. Each piece has a texture that calls out to be touched – the stippled sheen of the bare wood, the fluid weave of linen-upholstered armchairs, the silky weight of a loomed throw. Built-in bookcases add a hint of color beneath the windows and bring a finishing touch to the room's harmonious blend of airiness and depth.

Textural contrast, *right,* in a bedroom with plenty of windows and built-in storage, comes from light linen draperies hung floor-to-ceiling to create a dramatic scrim. When closed, the drapes make a clean sweep, muting the shelving without completely hiding it.

Even the smallest nook can become an impromptu vanity with the addition of a mirror. Here, woven baskets neatly store necessities on two low shelves in a built-in bookcase.

Design Details

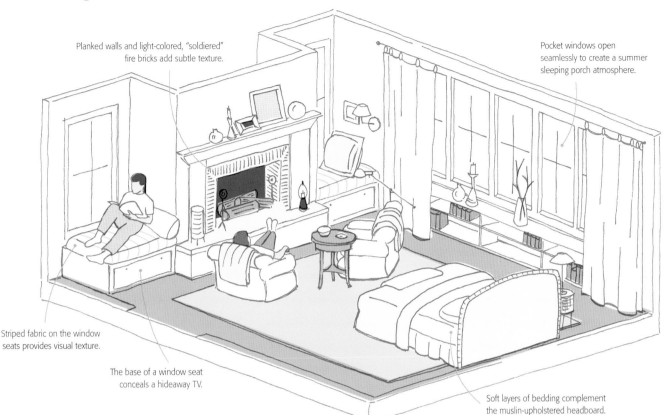

Planked walls and light-colored, "soldiered" fire bricks add subtle texture.

Pocket windows open seamlessly to create a summer sleeping porch atmosphere.

Striped fabric on the window seats provides visual texture.

The base of a window seat conceals a hideaway TV.

Soft layers of bedding complement the muslin-upholstered headboard.

Color Palette

In this all-white room, the bed is a perfect example of how to mix warm and cool whites. The bed skirt and sheets are a cool, crisp shade of white, while the upholstered headboard is a creamier shade. Cool whites are tinged with blue or gray; warm whites show hints of red or amber. In this case, the balance tips toward the warm side of the spectrum with the addition of honey-toned wood floors and a sandy-colored coir rug.

Room Plan

Monochromatic schemes, especially in white, are a good way to bring tranquility and visual organization to a busy space. In this bedroom, where everything is in its place, the cohesive color scheme emphasizes the serenity and natural logic of the floor plan. Closing the curtains hides the bookshelves. The stripes on the window seat upholstery mimic the vertical bricks in the fireplace, and a floating shelf serves as a bedside table. Built-in cubbies and drawers under one window seat make it easier to keep clutter at bay. The other window seat holds the TV.

Materials

Coir Beaten coconut fiber is spun and woven into patterns like this jacquard design. The color varies based on harvest time.

Faux fur This luxurious, plush material is completely synthetic and is as soft and warm as the real thing.

Mercury glass Silver coloring coats the inside of this double-walled glass, also called silvered glass. The coating is actually silver nitrate, which replaced the mercury used previously.

Timeless Texture

Imperfections often make things more beautiful, and some surfaces grow lovelier with age: worn paint, weathered metal, and vintage fabrics. As these materials show signs of seasoning, their charm only multiplies. The patina of age brings rich texture to any bedroom.

There's an uncommon beauty to worn surfaces that have been polished by decades of use. Paint becomes variegated and reveals subtle undertones; metal takes on a darker, richer hue; fabrics grow soft; wall coverings fade to sepia hues. If the floors, walls, or furnishings of your bedroom have vintage appeal, consider using them as a starting point for layering the space with a palette of aged textures.

Sometimes the shape and style of a room itself can inspire a texture palette. Small rooms – especially attic bedrooms like this one – often demand imaginative solutions. The deep eaves and irregular angles of this bedroom called for an asymmetrical furniture arrangement centered on a simple metal bedstead, allowing the bed to take center stage and set the tone for the room's decor. Angled into the space from a corner, the open silhouette of the antique frame lets the surrounding textures of wall covering, bed linens, and silk striped voile window panels shine through.

Twin distressed old chests echo the bed's antique appeal. With a bureau scarf matched to the bed skirt, one chest displays a simple textured still life: metal, glazed ceramic, clear glass, and ruffled blossoms.

Crackled with age, *left*, an antique iron bedstead becomes a frame for a crisp taffeta bed skirt. Bed skirts are a simple way to inject pattern, color, and seasonal interest into a room. **Silk striped voile panels**, *right*, have been informally tacked to the windows for a casual look.

Layers of texture suggest history.
A combination of old linens, silk taffeta,
matelassé, and sheer silk, plus pillows
and throws, invite you to settle in.

White makes an ideal foil for worn surfaces, especially in the bedroom. It suggests softness, and suffuses the space with light, which accentuates the room's rich texture. White also subtly unifies mismatched shapes and materials. It can bring an eclectic mix of furnishings together comfortably and harmoniously.

Look for white-painted wood and metal to provide some grace notes of texture in a bedroom. Metal bedsteads, which first came into fashion during the mid-eighteenth century (when the industrial revolution made iron a popular furnishing material), introduce a welcome structural element to a room without adding bulk. Layered with fine white bedding and flanked by twin chests, this beautifully weathered bed frame seems to float out from the corner of the room.

Like the distressed floorboards and the painting found at a flea market, the antique fluted chests with their richly carved legs introduce an elegant sense of history. Symmetrically placed and topped with matching lamps, they lend the room a casual structure.

A stack of vintage throws, blankets, and fabric of antique wool flannel, chenille, channel-stitched cotton, matelassé, and lambswool has old-fashioned charm. Furnishings and accessories found at flea markets are often rich in unique aged textures, and decorating with them is a creative way to express your personal style.

Design Details

Color Palette

This carefully edited space displays a symphony of creamy off-whites and whites. The presence of sage green and deep pink instantly gives life to the room, drawing in the eye and suggesting a natural freshness. When using only a small amount of color in an otherwise neutral decor, the use of complements adds impact. (Complementary colors are those that fall directly opposite each other on the color wheel: red and green, yellow and purple, blue and orange.) Deep pink stands out more vividly when paired with its complement, green.

Materials

Painted wood floor It was common in the eighteenth century to paint hand-hewn and uneven floorboards to give them a uniform appearance. A painted floor can unify an entire room through the use of color.

Metal bed frame Metals such as iron give a bed structure without bulk. Modern options include steel and cast aluminum, a combination that's stronger and lighter than its iron predecessors. Also, finishes can mimic the look of a desired metal, such as brass, without the maintenance hassles.

Taffeta The lustrous sheen of taffeta, whether it's made from cotton or silk, makes this lightweight fabric a luxurious choice for window treatments, table skirts, and bed skirts. Often woven in a plaid pattern, taffeta is traditionally used for ball gowns and formal fashions.

Pulling a room together using imperfect pieces is an exercise in creativity. Experiment with color and texture. A vase of flowers brightens a simple desk, braided rugs enrich waxed white floorboards, and linen towels cover a multitude of surfaces. To take the look in a contemporary direction, add new fashion accessories for a fresh counterpoint, giving the room a sophisticated air.

Mismatched chairs, *left*, reinforce the "found" appeal of this attic room. Layering textures and mixing furniture styles make this an intimate bedroom that reveals a stong sense of personality in its choices. **Old mirror glass**, *above*, can have a mottled or gold cast that complements distressed furnishings and heirlooms.

Soft flooring

In a bedroom, it's especially important to consider how every texture will feel against your skin. In a space where you want to feel soothed and nurtured, a soft rug underfoot can be an inspiring way to start each day. Choose the softest materials for bedroom rugs – lambswool, silk chenille, or cotton shag.

Tufted wool Practical for high-traffic areas, wool's dense weave makes the surface difficult for dirt to penetrate.

Shag When you want the comfort and warmth of a high-pile rug and eye-catching style, shag is ideal.

Chenille Woven of cotton, silk, or a blend, chenille often is used for braided rugs. It offers superior softness, density, and sheen.

Soft furnishings

The padded shapes of beds, chaise longues, ottomans, and pillows have a natural bias toward softness. Make them even more inviting by adding layers of texture and lush upholstery fabrics like velvet. To enhance the appeal of bedroom furnishings and highlight their comfort, choose textiles that call out to be touched.

Cotton This natural fabric, especially Egyptian cotton, softens with washing.

Velvet Rows of raised pile loops are cut to enhance velvet's furry texture. Lush and sensuous, velvet is ideal for bedroom duvets and pillows.

Leather A fine choice for chairs and headboards, smooth leather and suede (napped leather) have natural warmth and soften with wear.

Soft accessories

Luxuriously soft textures and materials are a must for any bedroom. The key is finding soft textures that are appropriate for each purpose – as bed linens, decorative pieces, and practical accents. Comfort is the most important element in this room, so choose a soft yet appropriate material for each accessory that you add to the room.

Faux fur Perfect for throw blankets and pillows, faux fur adds a playful accent or a stylish alternative to wool.

Silk Strong and warm, yet lightweight and liquidy soft, all-season silk is as practical and affordable as cotton.

Percale Whether it's all cotton or a cotton/polyester blend, percale is tightly woven to create a soft material that softens more with each washing.

soft and hard textures for your bedroom

Hard flooring

The benefit of hard floors – whether wood, tile, stone, or concrete – is that they are easy to keep clean. If you have pets or allergies to dust or mold, hard flooring is frequently your best option. While these materials are not as soft underfoot as a carpet, you can warm them up by adding area rugs or by installing radiant heat beneath the floor.

Soft woods Less expensive than hardwoods, soft woods such as pine should be treated with heavy-duty finishes for more durability.

Hardwood Scratch-resistant and hardwearing, cherry, maple, and oak are examples of hardwoods.

Tile Terra-cotta or ceramic tiles are a way to transform your room and add textured sophistication to the floors.

Hard furnishings

Fine craftsmanship and lasting durability are the hallmarks of hard furnishings' appeal. Furniture made from carved or joined wood adds a feeling of warmth to the bedroom. Distressed wood furnishings have a well-worn, casual look. Hard furnishings balance the soft shapes of the bedroom and give the decor a substantial quality.

Painted wood Paint can update furniture. White and cream hues blend easily with other finishes; black is sophisticated; crackle glazes are rustic.

Stained wood Finishes from antique honey to traditional mahogany highlight the beauty of wood.

Wicker, caning, and rattan Flexible, sturdy open-weave construction is lighter and less bulky than wood.

Hard accessories

The solid nature of hard accessories adds a sculptural element to the bedroom. Whether made from metal, plastic, or porcelain, the shapes of hard accessories counter the abundance of soft elements like bedding, upholstery, pillows, and textiles. This balance of hard and soft textures gives a bedroom greater depth and dimension.

Glass Available in a myriad of colors and shapes, glass accessories' transparent or translucent surfaces offer glints of light and liquid beauty.

Ceramics Stoneware, porcelain, and pottery all have a handwrought look and wonderful tactile appeal.

Mirrors Polished or smooth reflective surfaces, typically glass, add utility and a sense of spaciousness to a room.

furnishings

Furnishings are the key pieces, fabrics, and accessories that make a bedroom what it is, but style is what makes it yours. Fill it with furniture and accents that engage the senses. Although many furnishings can create comfort – a chair for reading, a carpet to lounge on, a table to keep necessities nearby – a beautiful bedroom begins with its essential piece of furniture: a great bed. Its curves, posts, headboard, height, color, and materials all combine to set a tone for the room. Before you invest in any other furnishings, take time to choose a bed you love.

For additional bedroom furnishings, combine elements from different eras and provenances. Pair opposites; cross boundaries. Coupling an antique bed with contemporary side tables displays a modern sensibility that borrows from the past.

In a bedroom, seating can be clean and simple, but sumptuous is even better: chaise longues, club chairs, and overstuffed pillows in window seats. Bedside tables offer opportunities to add whimsy. Instead of a traditional nightstand, stack books or baskets to serve the same function, or repurpose a piece such as a crate or stool.

Furnish your bedroom for individual comfort with personal flair. Choose classic furniture, plush rugs, cushions, and fabrics. Add favorite keepsakes.

You can choose from a tremendous range of styles. Begin by considering the classics. Platform beds, true to their name, are simply that: stylish platforms for a mattress without headboard or footboard. Stately and romantic, canopy beds have been a royal staple for centuries (though peasants actually invented them). Four-poster beds add drama and visual height to a bedroom. Iron beds have the appeal of antiques and an airy framework that's especially suited to small spaces. The gentle curves and shapely proportions of a sleigh bed are perfect for a room with a bed as its centerpiece. Daybeds, ideal in a guest room, are actually sofas by day and beds when dusk falls.

Room to spare? Introduce an armoire, a tall, free-standing cupboard that predates the built-in closet by centuries. Originally designed to store arms and armor, armoires make handsome hide-aways for home theater systems, stereos, and other electronic equipment. They're tailor-made for storage and can even hold a small home office.

Well-chosen furnishings in different styles can happily coexist, but pieces look particularly attractive when they echo each other's features. Match the curve of a headboard with one atop an armoire, or a detail on a side table with one on a chair. Create your own classic combination for a comfortable arrangement that suits your style.

A Simple Change of Style

A classic bedroom can take on a completely different personality with a few quick changes in furnishings. This room works two ways: dressed up in light layers of vintage fabrics, it has a country cottage sensibility; dressed down, it makes a strong contemporary statement.

The world of furnishings offers countless opportunities for you to make changes, large and small, in your decor. But you don't have to replace major pieces to update the look of a bedroom. Classic furnishings – all the furniture and soft goods that you bring into a room – have an appeal that endures and can adapt to changing tastes in style.

If you're seeking a fresh look, you have several options. Repositioning furniture such as your bed is one option. Changing all the bed linens is another. A combination of the two gives a big impact with minimal effort: change and rearrange a few key pieces, and switch the style of bedding and other soft furnishings.

If you choose to rearrange, the shape of the room and the style of your bed will narrow your options. For instance, a room with low eaves simply won't accommodate a canopy or four-poster bed against its walls. You'll have to "float" the bed in the center of the space. This can be an advantage because it gives a bed a powerful sense of presence. You can also place a bed perpendicular to a wall to divide the room into two zones, as this room does.

A toile de Jouy–topped table, *left*, gives the room a romantic feel. Toile de Jouy, literally "fabric from Jouy," was first made in 1760 in Jouy-en-Josas, France. Its manufacturing process was revolutionary at the time because it allowed greater detail in printing. A homespun linen bolster, *right*, and a complementary American piecework quilt balance the toile with bold patterns.

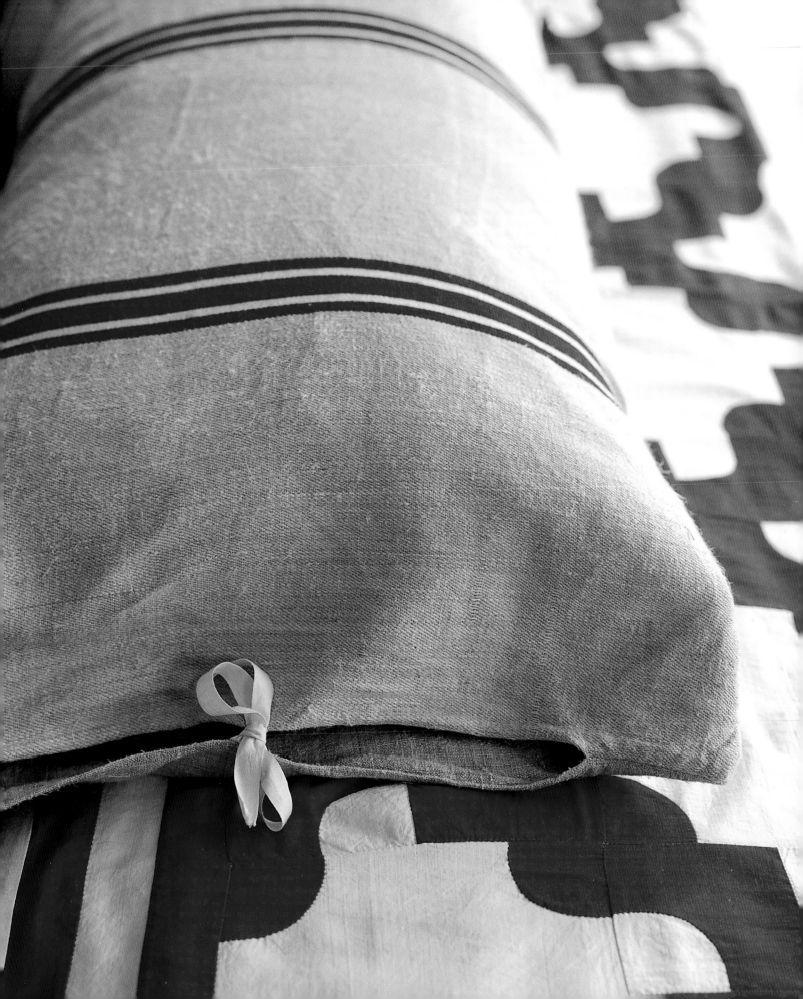

A deft use of fabrics brings a delicate quality to this room. European toile de Jouy is sewn together with gingham checks. Plaid kitchen towels are used as a runner to warm up a cabinet at the foot of the bed. A sheer expanse of voile covers a maple pedestal table with a light veil that allows its classic silhouette to show through.

Sleigh beds offer considerable leeway in bedroom decorating. Their sculptural lines are suited to many different room configurations and pair well with a variety of linens. Laid with simple white sheets, a sleigh bed is graphic and contemporary. Layered with patterns, it's sculptural and soft.

This modern sleigh-style bed, *left*, works well with both vintage and contemporary styling. Sleigh beds are so named for their resemblance to Victorian sleighs. **A crystal candlestick**, *above*, is fashioned into a bedside lamp with a crisp pleated shade.

You have lots of options when you're ready to give your bedroom a new look. You can vary pieces of furniture or entire groupings, switch accessories, or alter a color palette.

Here, the room is transformed by bringing in a classic leather armchair, moving a nightstand to the end of the bed, and changing the linens. The room's color scheme is changed entirely, and a completely different ambience emerges. With its fabrics and layers edited, the room gains a contemporary feel, opening itself up to the soaring eaves of the A-frame architecture.

In this pared-down space, the furnishings appear more prominent, and details play a more significant role in the decor. On the bed, gray linens and a mohair throw provide a restful base, allowing accents like the flower arrangement and red chair to attract the eye. The quieter palette draws attention toward the end of the room rather than focusing it on the bed. With a simple change of furnishings, this room adopts a dramatically different point of view.

En suite with the bath, *left*, this master bedroom adopts a look that emphasizes spaciousness. **A red leather club chair**, *right*, draws focus, offset by a Biedermeier-style table and tripod lamp. The lattice base of a folding table adds visual texture at the end of the bed.

Design Details

Color Palette

Red and white is one of the most arresting color combinations (picture the effect of a stop sign, with white letters popping off a bright red background). Used in interiors, the combination creates an eye-catching look. This bold bedroom features striking red-and-white graphic patterns in plaid, toile de Jouy, gingham, and stripes. A natural linen color, seen in a homespun bolster, tempers the palette and acts as a soothing neutral counterpoint.

Color Palette

Gray is a color chameleon; like white, it easily takes on different hues with changing light. It can appear blue or even lavender at different times of day. Gray and ivory together are a soft yet masculine combination. They have a calming effect akin to blue, but are more grounded. Accented with the mahogany tones of polished wooden furniture, this appealingly contemporary palette offers the perfect neutral backdrop for a few brightly colored accessories.

Materials

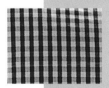

Gingham This lightweight cotton fabric feels like the very definition of Americana, but in fact it originally came from India. The classic red-and-white checkerboard pattern was an American enhancement.

Natural linen Woven from the flax plant, this breathable fabric has a naturally nubby texture that softens with age. Vintage linen pieces contribute a sense of history.

Materials

Leather Tanned animal hides make a durable upholstery option that gets softer and more beautiful with use. Leather takes on a contemporary look when dyed a bright color, such as this cherry red.

Flat-weave wool Smoothly finished with no knots or pile, flat-weave wool provides a durable, insulating rug. This neutral canvas makes the room adaptable to new styles.

Furnishing a Guest Room

Guest bedrooms require creative, adaptable design. When friends aren't visiting, the room should be a useful part of the home. When they come to call, it should be inviting and thoughtfully designed. The right fabrics and furniture combine the best of both worlds comfortably and neatly.

Space is a luxury, but if you're clever, an extra guest room can keep both you and your guests in the utmost comfort. If you have an extra room, you probably use it regularly, with or without company. A guest room often doubles as a home office, den, playroom, or even storage room. A versatile approach helps you get the most out of the space, and makes your guests feel the room has been designed entirely to meet their needs and enhance their enjoyment.

Begin with adaptable furnishings – pieces that are as suited to living areas as they are to sleeping spaces. If the room is also used as a home office, for example, furnish it with a table that's a comfortable working height rather than a desk. Choose shapes and accessories with neatly tailored lines, such as a classic pedestal table that can double as a nightstand, a chair that provides comfortable support but doesn't look like it's at work, and storage pieces that are at home in living spaces as well as bedrooms. In dual-purpose rooms, an ironwork daybed is a hardworking choice for a guest bed, offering a place to sleep and to sit.

Invite repose, *left*, with an abundance of pillows in matelassé, ticking pattern, and brightly colored piecework. A versatile palette of creams and whites is a winning combination for rooms that both entertain guests and encourage home-office work. **The daybed**, *right*, was a popular seating choice in seventeenth-century France, where it was called a *lit de repos* (a bed for a short rest). The bedside table is a moveable piece that allows a leisurely breakfast and converts to a work surface if the room doubles as an office.

A multipurpose room fills up quickly, especially if it's used as a part-time office. If you can separate the room into two zones, one for work and one for guests, it will help keep things organized. When visitors are expected, stow away your paperwork and leave notecards, pens, writing pads, and maps on the desk.

Make a work room feel like a bedroom when guests arrive: add fresh flowers, of course, and soft pillows and throws to encourage napping.

This room asked for a balance of privacy and intimacy, so linen panels were hung as an informal divider. The drapes soften the architecture of the space and give it an airy feel. This spaciousness, enhanced by the light, restful palette, creates an atmosphere equally suited to working and relaxing. You could also use a screen or bookshelves as a divider.

Placing the bed by the window, *left*, highlights the elegant ironwork. A looped shag rug is a wonderful luxury under bare feet, and the neutral tone works well for a low-traffic space. **The open frame of the table base**, *right*, lets light flow through the room. The floor is acid-stained cement, sealed for durability.

Choose guest room furnishings that impart warmth and grace, and add thoughtful, personal accents that make your visitors feel special.

Both guest rooms and offices require clever storage ideas and intelligent planning. Here, a double-door armoire cleanly divides storage for guest and office essentials. One side is furnished with a robe and slippers, warm throws, and extra blankets; the other keeps files and paperwork out of sight. Lined with striped wallpaper, the armoire is attractive whether left open or closed. The repetition of crisp stripes throughout the room is cheerful and appropriate both for bedrooms and offices.

A stack of hatboxes has been arranged alongside the bed to fashion a witty nightstand. Roomy enough on top to hold bedside necessities, the hatboxes also provide three times more storage than a standard bedside table and enhance the room's visual appeal.

Neatly striped bed linens, *left*, look as tailored as a dress shirt. **An armoire**, *right*, provides ample closet space for guest necessities. Using patterned paper lining or unexpected color on the insides of doors, closets, or drawers gives a finished look and is a pleasant surprise for visitors.

A small dressing area, just outside a sheer curtain divide, is set up for guests. Show off a special antique quilt by hanging it as artwork. Choose quilts with large patterns and bold colors for maximum impact.

Design Details

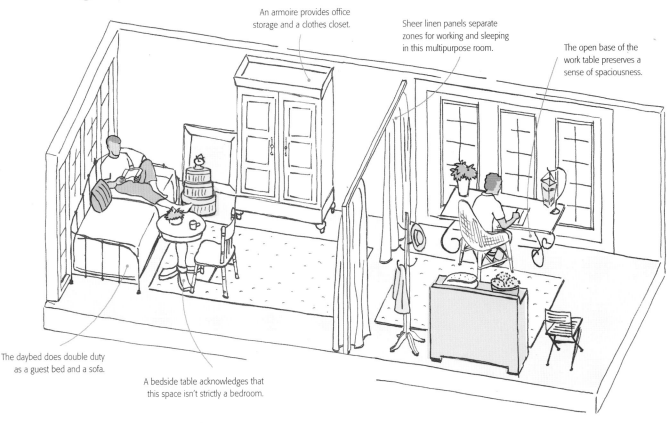

An armoire provides office storage and a clothes closet.

Sheer linen panels separate zones for working and sleeping in this multipurpose room.

The open base of the work table preserves a sense of spaciousness.

The daybed does double duty as a guest bed and a sofa.

A bedside table acknowledges that this space isn't strictly a bedroom.

Color Palette

The clever placement of just a few bold colors energizes a neutral palette in this combination guest room and home office. Here, sun-drenched, faded brights provide colorful accents in a space filled with creamy whites and beige stripes. A pale blue painted commode and touches of red, pink, and orange – in the hanging piecework quilt and on the bed – break up the reign of neutrals and add splashes of lighthearted fun.

Room Plan

An unexpected combination of painted wood furniture makes the most of this multipurpose guest room. A tea table and chair are pulled up to a wrought-iron daybed for a sleeping space that doubles as a breakfast nook and conversation area. An old painted armoire, an oversized counterpoint to the other furniture in the room, serves as a home-office storage area and a guest closet. Separated by sheer drapes, the front half of the space acts as a home office and a dressing area. French doors provide outdoor access.

Materials

Shag rug A soft, deep pile makes shag rugs a comfy underfoot option for a bedroom with casual style.

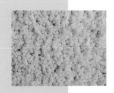

Cement Recent innovations in dyeing and tinting allow cement slab floors to be made in any color and even etched with designs.

Striped cotton Pinstripes give bedding a haberdashery style as tailored as a dress shirt. Natural and breathable, cotton bedding gets softer with repeated washings.

How to Dress a Bed

The shape of the bed and the style of its linens set the tone for a bedroom. For a romantic and sensual atmosphere, consider a shapely iron bed or a settee-style daybed that invites lounging on soft pillows. For a modern take, choose a solid headboard or platform bed topped with a lofty duvet. If you prefer casual, rustic charm, opt for a painted wooden bed and drape it with colorful quilts. If you want maximum flexibility for the style of your bedroom, an upholstered headboard can be slipcovered easily to fashion a new look.

A graceful iron bed, *left*, veiled with a simple canopy of netting, looks regal and elegant. Embroidered linens, stacked pillows, and a shimmering silk cushion make the bed appear sumptuous. The airy silhouette of iron beds lets you use queen-sized beds or tall headboards in small spaces or in front of windows without sacrificing spaciousness or blocking out light.

The same room takes a graphic stance, *above*, with the simple form of an aniline-dyed wooden headboard and pastel linens. The geometry of the tailored plaid duvet and pillowcases keeps the bed crisp and uncluttered.

A classic farmhouse bed, *right*, with its painted wood headboard, is a sturdy, flexible choice. The postage-stamp quilt is a traditional American design. Simple beds like this are also a good bet for children's rooms, because they can be fitted with a pull-out trundle, an invention that doubles the bed space for sleepovers.

How to Reinvent a Nightstand

Bedside tables don't have to be designed specifically for the bedside. In fact, anything can serve the same purpose – a dining chair, a stack of books, an upturned antique crate, or a floating wall shelf installed for easy reach. For years, a bed flanked by two nightstands has been part of the standard suite of bedroom furniture. Why not turn the tables, so to speak, and show your personal flair? As long as there's enough surface area to hold bedside necessities, almost anything goes, the more imaginative the better. You can also try different placements for your piece – at the foot of the bed, for example – if space is at a premium.

A chair is often all you need, *left*, to hold essentials, especially in a child's room. As a bonus, it can be handily whisked away for extra seating when needed. **A Moroccan tea table**, *far left, top*, is slightly higher than a standard nightstand, but its intricate open framework and hexagonal shape give a hint of exotic flavor. **Stacked hatboxes and suitcases**, *below left*, are not only charming but also offer more storage capacity than a classic bedside table. All kinds of objects, when sturdily stacked, can be converted into a perfect nightstand.

This vintage red safe, *above*, works well because its proportions are similar to those of a standard bedside table. **A wooden desk**, *above right*, does double duty as a nightstand and a work area. **Stacked metal trunks**, *right*, freshly painted with white enamel, provide sleek storage and a large surface for accessories.

lighting

Bedroom lighting can be so much more than just having a lamp for reading at bedtime. The placement and intensity of lighting affects a space's atmosphere, making it cozy or cool, dramatic or cheerful. This is as true in a room that demands darkness for a third of its life as anywhere else in the house. How you light the room where you sleep and wake will affect your everyday moods as well as your sleep habits.

The right level of light in a bedroom is entirely personal. Lighting that seems dim to one person may seem soothing to another. Whatever your

shadows and glare. For a quick improvement to overhead lights, switch to a pink bulb and install a dimmer switch, an inexpensive and easy fix that lets you raise or lower the wattage as needed.

Task lighting is focused light that illuminates a specific activity. Wall-mounted swing-arm lamps, crookneck pharmacy lamps, and other spot-focus lamps are all task lights. Available in a vast number of styles, task lamps offer both direct illumination and great design flexibility because you often can change their style and the effects of their light with different shades or positioning.

Gently filtered and flattering light in a bedroom creates a sense of calm and repose. By day, abundant natural light brings in energy and warmth.

requirements, the placement and intensity of illumination in a bedroom should be flexible enough to let you read, work, and relax comfortably.

There are three kinds of lighting to consider: ambient (or general), task (or spot), and accent. Ambient lighting, like the diffused sunlight outdoors, is overall lighting – the kind you hardly think about because it's all around. It is the light cast by overhead fixtures, whether recessed and largely invisible (as in most modern houses) or pendant and decorative (as in older homes).

When planning this layer of light, think like a photographer: you want illumination that's complementary, soft, and evenly diffused to minimize

Accent lights are specific and attention-grabbing. They're used to set mood, draw focus, or add sparkle. Larger accent lights like wall washers impart a soft, colorful glow; spotlights can draw attention to favorite artwork or emphasize a focal wall; flickering candles create a sense of movement and cast dramatic shadows.

Don't forget daylight when making your lighting plan. Let natural light and lamplight work in harmony. Try golden-colored lamp shades to brighten cloudy days. Use mirrors and other reflective surfaces to increase light in the room and give it play. Remember, this isn't just the room you sleep in, it's where you wake up, too.

Creating Drama with Light

As a determiner of mood, light has no rival. It's the trick up the sleeve of every successful theatrical designer. For bedroom light that's soft and flattering, borrow a simple secret of set design: veil the light with translucent fabric scrims to make the room glow.

Decorating with light is more than a matter of choosing lamps and fixtures. The way you control the lighting is just as important to the style of a room. Bright light creates an atmosphere of energy and motion. Low light is restful and romantic. Simply by screening light with easily sewn panels of sheer fabric (or scrims, as they are called in stage design), you can alter light and bathe a space in a warm glow.

Scrims are used in the world of theater to set a stage. When light is cast upon them from the front, they act as delicate, opaque dividers. When lit from behind, they become translucent. Scrims offer a way to veil a sleeping area, yet retain a sense of openness. Hung floor-to-ceiling, they fashion a translucent pavilion around the bed. This room cleverly employs scrims to shape space and diffuse illumination. In the shared space of this bedroom, long voile panels were added to soften the transition between working and sleeping areas and lend an exotic air. The room's textures and colors reflect light in their own unique ways. Iridescent and metallic accents mingle with shimmery silk pillows and crisp, gold-embroidered bed linens.

Sheer fabric panels, *left,* were attached along their top edges to the bookcase with lengths of Velcro. They are dramatically brought to life by under-cabinet halogen lamps. This bedroom required a flexible, multipurpose lighting plan that fostered work and inspiration. Low-voltage pillar lights are unobtrusive bookends by day, glimmering accents by night. **Simple, romantic scrims,** *right,* surround a platform bed.

Before you install scrims, understand how light behaves in your room. If the room is naturally bright, you may wish to use more opaque gauze or linen fabric (instead of voile) to screen it. If light remains low throughout the day, you may need to add light so the scrims will appear translucent. Also consider manipulating light to define separate areas. You can use slightly brighter light to subtly stake out territory for work and creativity, and lower light in areas dedicated to rest and relaxation.

To create the effect shown here, three floor-to-ceiling lengths of voile, in melon and soft pink, were hemmed on all sides, attached to wooden dowels at top and bottom, and suspended from the ceiling. The sheer panels separate the bed from the desk, shield the work area from glare, and minimize bright light around the sleeping area. The rice-paper pendant light is deliberately overscaled to create a soft-focus glow centered on the bed.

Add a light touch, *left*, with white and pale pink bed linens and silk shibori pillows to balance the rich colors of wood and walls. **A wood-and-metal apothecary lamp**, *right*, provides task light for the desk and reveals a shapely silhouette and a glint of light when viewed through the scrim.

Natural light is changeable through the day, so a lighting plan needs to complement it accordingly, especially if you want to experiment with scrims. When the sun's angle is low, natural light through the windows and doors hits the sheer panels of the scrims, creating an impression of many intersecting planes of light. Adding controlled lighting determines the panels' effects.

Soft lighting instantly infuses a room with romance. Filtered through lengths of fabric, daylight becomes as shimmering and warm as a sunrise.

All types of lighting have been layered into this room. Ambient light comes from the recessed ceiling fixtures and the rice-paper pendant light. Table and desk lamps provide task lighting in work areas. Accent lights abound, with picture lights, bookcase lamps, under-cabinet halogen lamps, votives, pillar candles, and candle lanterns peppered throughout the space.

Desk lamps, *left*, need not be ordinary to be effective. This one is fashioned from a music-stand base; a vinyl shade adds warmth to its light. Well-placed accent lights, *right*, like these frosted glass pillars and votive candles, bring an exotic glow to the room.

Design Details

Accent lights extend the full length of the shelves, adding drama to the wall.

Translucent scrims screen the work area from window glare.

A desktop task lamp casts a bright circle of downward light.

Lanterns and candlelight change the mood for evening relaxation.

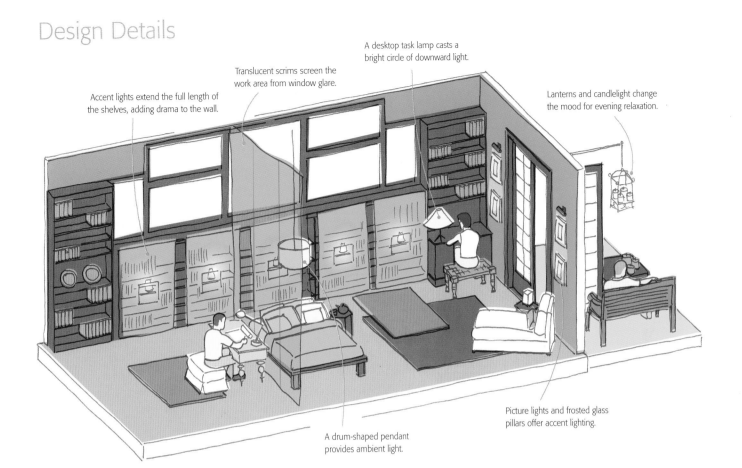

A drum-shaped pendant provides ambient light.

Picture lights and frosted glass pillars offer accent lighting.

Color Palette

The inspiration for this bedroom's exotic color scheme comes from eastern Asia, where colors are often used at full saturation to stand up to brilliant sunlight and deep shadows. Adjacent colors in the spectrum, orange and pink shades blend and overlap with the deep crimson on the walls to create an energy-filled, warm atmosphere awash with color and light. Because the pink and orange hues have equal intensity, they harmonize.

Room Plan

Translucent scrims and a careful lighting plan carve out different zones within this colorful bedroom. A scrim of three panels divides a functional work area, with its own desktop task lighting, from the rest of the space. More scrims hide bookcases, keeping work and rest separate. The rice-paper lantern hung low over the platform bed is controlled with a floor switch that adjusts reading and ambient lighting for the sleeping area. Layered area rugs further define zones and add comfort and warmth. A candlelit patio extends the living area outside.

Materials

Kilims Originally designed to be placed on sandy desert floors, these richly patterned flat-weave rugs feature vibrant geometric patterns.

Voile This crisp, finely woven fabric is traditionally made from cotton or silk, but can also be wool or synthetic. Light plays off its sheerness.

Shibori silk This Japanese fabric art is often likened to tie-dyeing, but shibori requires greater precision because silk is so absorbent.

Lighting for Ambience

Give a bedroom an ethereal atmosphere with colored bulbs, candlelight, and crystal. Use etched mirrors, clear glass, and translucent fabrics to play with light and shadow.

In a bedroom designed for mood and enchantment, lighting is a key design element. A blend of lush textures – satin, silk, and faux chinchilla – takes on added depth and dimension when dramatically lit with chandeliers and candlelight.

Windows swathed in sheer drapes permit natural light to fill the room by day and add a touch of mystery at night. Sheer voile veils a simple wooden armchair for a gossamer touch of glamour.

A sculptural vignette of candles and oil lamps, *above*, shimmers on a marble-topped table. A silvery Venetian mirror, *right*, refracts light with its faceted surfaces. The draperies are hung to create a faux canopy. A chandelier, *opposite*, casts a flattering glow with a soft pink bulb.

How to Create Mood with Candles

Make every day glow with candlelight. Candles are an inspired accent, especially in the haven of a bedroom. Just a few can bathe the room in beauty and variety with their subtle color, scent, and warm, clear light. Use constellations of candlelight to create a peaceful sanctuary in your bedroom at the end of a long day. Encircle candles with glass or crystals to capture the spirit of Old World chandeliers; tuck shells or flowers next to them for an instant celebration of nature. A single candle suggests volumes: the warmth of the hearth and the twinkle of the night sky, all contained in a flickering, tapered flame.

Enhance a flame's glow, *above*, by standing candles in large glass vases or hurricanes. Place them up high on shelves or low to the ground to cast a spell of flickering light at every level. **Votive candles**, *right*, are unobtrusive by day and utterly transforming when lit in the evening. Arranged at table height across a room, they gild the entire space with a soft field of light. Mirrors and glass accessories multiply votives' reflections. Or, use a string of fairy lights along the edge of a shelf to produce the same sparkle without the flame.

Floating candles, *left*, are made with wax that contains trapped air bubbles. They offer the surprise of the unexpected – floating fire on water – and give flower arrangements nighttime dazzle. **Match materials to mood**, *below*, and nest candles in glass or crystal beads for effervescent sparkle. Try using sea glass, shells, pebbles, or even a stylist's trick: dried beans. Beans come in many sizes and colors, and make interesting and decorative stabilizers surrounding a candle base.

Find Your Style A select guide to choosing and using the best

Ambient lighting

Ambient lighting is the main illumination in a room. It may come from several fixtures, from a single ceiling-mounted fixture, or as natural sunlight coming through the windows. Ambient light makes a space welcoming by filling it with a warm, general wash of light. By day, ambient light may be a combination of natural and artificial light. Incandescent bulbs in translucent glass ceiling fixtures disperse warm, flattering light. By night, a bedroom calls for ambient lighting that's adjustable for relaxing and reading and that can be completely blocked for sleeping.

Wall-mounted uplight

Task lighting

Task lighting is the light that helps you read and work in the bedroom. It focuses on particular areas and can be introduced either with moveable lamps or with fixed styles such as pendants and sconces. Most bedrooms require effective task lighting next to the bed as well as in reading corners, at vanities, and on work surfaces. When planning task lighting, think about the proximity of the light to the task area and how the material and color of the lamp shade will affect the light.

Table lamp

Accent lighting

Accent lights help you create drama and mood in a bedroom, whether with the soft glow of a nightlight or the sparkle of candlelight. More decorative than utilitarian, an accent light relies on the power of illumination to attract attention to an object. Often, it can be a beautiful decorative accessory on its own. Use accent lighting to spotlight a photo, collection, or display. Place accent lights in bookcase shelves or on a long mantel for subtle illumination. In the bedroom, candles are the ultimate accent lights; use them to fill the room with a soft glow.

Nightlight

ambient, task, and accent lighting for your bedroom

Torchière

Pendant

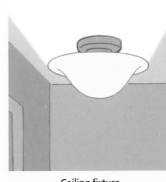

Ceiling fixture

Wall-mounted uplights or sconces cast a diffused glow and are wise choices for pale-colored rooms or reflective wall finishes.

Torchières are also uplights; their beam bounces from the ceiling before angling down.

Pendants hang from the ceiling, providing good background light. Adjust light levels with dimmers.

Ceiling fixtures can be recessed or mounted flush to the ceiling.

Swing-arm lamp

Desk lamp

Closet light

Table lamps with three-way bulbs allow for adjustable levels of light in the bedroom.

Swing-arm lamps, perfect at the bedside, provide light that can be directed as needed.

Desk lamps focus a bright, downward beam of light with a high level of illumination.

Closet lights come in options such as hard-wired, low-voltage, or battery-operated.

Candle

Beaded-shade lamp

Mini-chandelier

Nightlights are very low wattage and offer illumination by which to navigate or sleep.

Candles create an atmosphere of relaxation and calmness. They can also subtly scent a room.

Beaded-shade lamps change the quality of light, tinting it with jewel tones.

Mini-chandeliers hang from the ceiling. Their prisms refract light around the room.

windows

For some people, the greatest asset to any bedroom is a flood of sunlight streaming through floor-to-ceiling windows. For others, the sheltered atmosphere created by heavy curtains drawn sash to ceiling provides comfort. Windows are portals between our private worlds and what lies beyond, and the treatments you choose to cover them define their effect.

The variety of blinds, drapes, shades, shutters, and valances available can seem nearly endless. Luckily, dressing your windows isn't solely about style. Practical concerns help narrow the options.

with diaphanous fabrics. Express your whimsical side with brighter colors, patterns, or vintage fabrics. Dress a room down with casual match-stick bamboo blinds, or add classic architectural interest with wide wooden shutters.

With all the beautiful hardware available for hanging drapes, the jewelry of window treatments has become just as important as the coverings themselves. Choose hardware that makes opening and closing drapes or blinds effortless, then add decorative hardware with tiebacks, finials, and finishes that complement the room's decor.

Windows are a natural focal point. Whether airy and open or dramatically draped, the treatments you choose define the style and mood of your room.

When selecting window treatments, first consider how much privacy and how much light you want, then choose a flexible setup. A classic three-tiered system combines a light-blocking roller blind with sheer panels and heavier drapes hung on a double rod. This allows you to adjust the exposure according to the time of day: sheers at midday to diffuse the sun (perhaps with the blind partly drawn), and the blind and curtains pulled in the evening for a sense of enclosure.

Window treatments are practical necessities, but they're also an essential finishing touch. They offer another opportunity to add dimension to your room. Heighten an impression of softness

Windows welcome the unexpected. Dress them in ways that play against type. Hang embroidered velvet drapes in a casually styled bedroom. Mount sleek wooden shutters in an ornately decorated space. Introduce panels of brightly hued sheers to an otherwise neutral-toned room.

With their built-in frames, windows make a natural focal point for display. Take advantage of this fact and use a window to showcase a collection of colored bottles, found botanicals, or family photos. String translucent objects, sea glass, or prisms from the moulding to catch the light. Treated as something special, windows brighten a room as they welcome the world inside.

How to Drape a Window

When it comes to drapes, a layered look delivers the most options. Besides allowing good light control, layering is a creative way to bring color and contrast to bedroom windows. Using two sets of drapes lets you mix and match colors and textures. Pair an inner sheer with a rich outer layer of velvet or silk, or match hues to create a tone-on-tone effect. Begin by measuring the window and choosing a rod length and mounting height (consult the guide on pages 134–35). You can mount rods directly to the window frame or to the wall above it, depending on the look you want to achieve.

For a striking butterfly effect, *above,* treat the inner drapery layers as if they were linings and pin them back together, attaching them to the outer drapes. Double layers of dupioni silk are ideal for this treatment; their fluid surface makes them easy to align, and the fine weave has a rich, polished sheen. **A shapely silhouette,** *right,* is created by hanging drapes on a single curtain rod, then cinching them in the middle with a tie of chiffon. This style allows light in along the sides of the window, and it can be easily let out for more coverage. Hang the inner panel directly from the rod; attach the outer layer to the rod with sliding clip rings.

In an asymmetrical arrangement, a velvet outer layer sweeps over a panel of embroidered voile. Two velvet panels hang on the outer rod, pulled aside with a pepperberry beaded holdback. For asymmetrical treatments, the outer drapes should be gathered rather loosely so they cover more than half the window. Use a single panel for the inner layer, pulled neat and flat across the window, to let in light.

How to Give a Window a Light Touch

Bedroom window treatments must balance privacy and light, but some rooms just can't get enough of the latter. If your sleeping space needs as much illumination as it can get, treat your windows with a lighter touch. White cotton voile, linen, and organdy are known for superb draping and an ability to softly filter light. Or, just dress your windows with a simple valance, a breezy café curtain, or a stylish Roman shade. For very small windows, abandon fabric altogether and use textured, translucent paper – or place collections of glass items or objects from nature on the sill and use the window as a naturally lit display area.

Embroidery on soft Roman folds, *above*, adds structure and shape to a single sheer curtain panel. The panel is simply draped over the top of the rod and tacked at intervals to create an airy profile in an easily adjustable treatment. **A yardstick**, *right*, makes a witty alternative to a standard curtain rod. A crisp, simple panel is attached with cleverly fashioned metal rings and clips. **Treat windows boldly but simply**, *opposite,* with the clean lines and easy control of Roman shades. These are mounted inside the window frames, giving the mouldings more prominence.

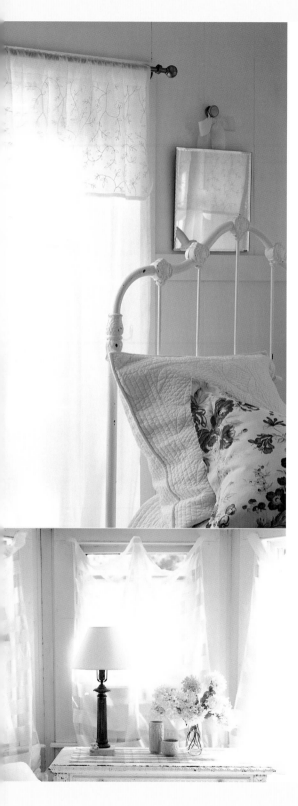

Curtains and drapes

Window treatments affect the amount of light that a bedroom receives, frame its view, and hide or enhance the shape of its windows. Sheer fabrics like voile, organdy, and linen filter light and offer a casual look. Rich fabrics like velvet, silk, and chenille block light; their shapely folds look more formal. The style and material of the rod, and the way the drape attaches to it, also influence your window style.

Rods are usually mounted 4" above the window (A); to add visual height to a room, mount the rod even higher. Or, you can mount the rod at the top of the frame (B). To determine the length of drape that you need, measure the length of your window, deciding where you want the drape to fall: to the sill (from A or B to C); below the sill (from A or B to D); or 1" above the floor (from A or B to E), which allows for clearance. To pool drapes on the floor, add 6–8".

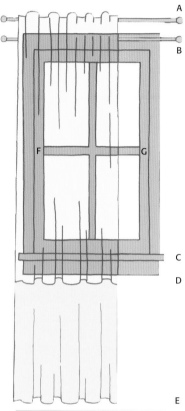

A Rod For *wall mount:* mount the curtain rod 4" above the window frame (A). For *trim mount:* mount the curtain rod at the top of the window frame (B). Extend the rod 1–3" on each side of the window frame as you please.

Width Measure the width of the window (F to G) and multiply that number by 1 for a tailored look, 1.5 for a standard look, or 3 for a full look.

C Length See the
D paragraph at left for instructions on measuring for length. When measuring, it's important to take into account the size of ring-tops, tie-tops, or other decorative tops, as they can add 1" or more to the length of a curtain or drapery panel.

Fabric panels

Fabric panels are easy, informal window treatments that can give a bedroom instant charm. They work equally well for light voiles and for heavier fabrics such as linen or canvas. Fabric panels can be tacked directly to a window frame, either in a looser, draped approach (*left*) or in a more formal, tailored fashion (*right*).

Tack the fabric directly to the window frame as shown.

Width Multiply the window width by 1 for a tailored look, 1.5 for a standard look, or 3 for a full look.

Length The panel can extend to the sill (B to C), below the sill (B to D), or to the floor (B to E).

drapery style for your bedroom windows

Rod To install ring-top or tie-top curtains or drapes, attach the curtain rod for wall mount (see the rod instructions at left). Extend the rod 3–4" on each side of the window, so the drapes can "stack back" to let in light. (Trim mounts are not well suited to this style, because light can show through the space between the rings.)

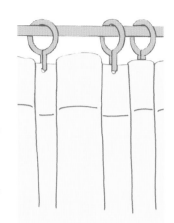

Ring-tops or tie-tops

This classic drapery and curtain treatment is wonderful for the bedroom because it allows window coverings to open and close with ease. Fullness suits this style: when measuring, multiply the window width by 3 and use two or more panels per side, as needed. Take the rings or ties into account when you measure for length, as they can add 1" or more to the top of the drapery panel.

Rod To install pole-pocket curtains, mount the curtain rod for trim mount or for wall mount (see the rod instructions at left). Extend the rod 1–3" on each side of the window frame.

Width Measure the window width (F to G) and multiply by 3; use two or more curtain panels per side, as needed.

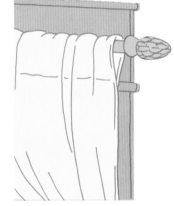

Pole-pocket rods

This style features a flat panel with a casing sewn at the top through which a rod can be inserted. Use ample fullness to allow the panel to shirr on the rod. Pole pockets are not as easy to slide along the rod as rings or tie-tops. However, most can be hung on drapery hooks, which attach to the pocket back and can be hung from rings. Decorative rod finials are a nice finishing touch.

Rod To install a double rod, mount the inner, lower curtain rod 1" above the window frame and 4" beyond each edge of the frame. The outer rod will be several inches above.

Length Take into account the rods' varying heights when measuring for length. The drape can extend below the sill (A to D) or to the floor (A to E).

Double rods

Multiply your options by installing a double rod. This lets you create a layered look with a sheer drape under a heavier drape. If the outer layer will be pulled back and the inner layer left as a screen for light, make the outer layer fuller to create drama when pulled back: when measuring, multiply the window width by 1.5 for a standard look (inner layer) or by 3 for a full look (outer layer).

storage

Everyone needs good storage, whether to create order, save space, or simply keep things within easy reach. In the bedroom, it's likely you'll need places to stow pillows and bedding, and to keep clothing and shoes neatly out of sight. But that's just the beginning. Today's bedrooms are used for more than just sleeping and dressing; they're often places for working, studying, entertaining, and even exercising. That's why well-planned storage is essential. Clever storage works with your habits. It accommodates routine and helps you stay organized.

Every bedroom is different, and luckily, storage solutions come in every shape, size, style, and color. To find storage that matches your needs and personal style, have a look at different options. Closed storage puts a lid on clutter; open solutions keep things at your fingertips. Freestanding storage can be moveable or fixed, ready to whisk out of sight, or there when you need it. Hanging storage, such as hooks, rings, and bars, helps keep things off the floor. Shelving is an ever-popular solution for those with limited floor space. It also offers flexibility: shelves can

The best storage can be decorative and personal as well as functional: it keeps essentials accessible and creates a sense of easy comfort in the bedroom.

In practical terms, this means storage should be placed at the level you naturally tend to put things: freestanding storage on the floor (like a hamper for clothes) or baskets on the nightstand (for books or papers). Designers often ask clients to note their daily habits and take these as cues for space planning. Try this trick yourself: keep track of where you put things down, then seek storage ideas fitted to just those places.

How do you want your bedroom to look? The answer greatly influences your storage strategies. Do you like to have everything in view, or would you prefer a streamlined look, banishing everything to drawers, cupboards, and closets?

be customized with baskets, tins, or other stylish containers to hold smaller items, and such decorative storage adds visual texture and warmth.

If visible storage isn't your style, bring in rolling storage drawers that fit under a bed. For a bedroom that's also a home office, a well-fitted armoire is a wise choice. It can be customized with a desk, bulletin board, and shelving and closed up entirely to hide work materials.

Whatever storage system you choose, design it with an eye toward the rest of the room's proportions and materials to create a harmonious whole. Storage is a fact of life. With a little imagination, it can be as beautiful as it is useful.

Small Solutions

Proving that creativity thrives wherever it is encouraged, space-saving storage around a cozy window seat creates an inviting nook for working, reading, or daydreaming.

"Condense and contain" is the motto of small-space living. If your bedroom needs storage with a bit of style and intimacy, a window seat might be just the solution.

If you have the right spot, a window seat is simple to build and furnish. With clever arranging, a nook can be fitted with everything you need. This alcove under the roofline of a bedroom is a cheerful spot to curl up in. Under-seat drawers, recessed shelves, adjustable lighting, and a handy filing rack within close reach make it a hardworking but easy-living space.

Built-in drawers, *far left and below*, take the role of a bureau, and stow away extra linens and clothing (but could easily hold office supplies). **Recessed shelving**, *center*, keeps essentials organized.

A Place for Everything

In any bedroom, finding artful ways of keeping belongings neat and tidy can be a challenge, especially in rooms where living space has been increased at the expense of closet space. Customized storage made from open shelving and soft containers offers a stylish solution.

It's wise to plan for twice as much storage space as you think you'll need. In new bedrooms, that's a tall order. The size of master suites has increased as bedrooms have grown into multipurpose spaces (with areas for lounging and working), demanding nearly as much square footage as living rooms once did. These open-plan spaces are inviting, light-filled, and, sometimes, a bit short on closet space.

If you're trying to expand storage options without crowding the room, look for furniture that either has a built-in storage capacity or that lends itself to holding containers. If the room has an open, airy atmosphere, you'll want storage styled to match and to integrate seamlessly.

Keeping storage items all white is a design trick that works well. Unified by a clean wash of white, storage fades into the background, and blends with white mouldings and trim. White has other benefits, too: most storage pieces are available in white, so it's easy to create an all-white system; it harmonizes beautifully with natural materials like seagrass and jute; and it makes a bedroom feel clean and restful.

The top of a bookshelf headboard, *left*, is both decorative and functional. It supplies a display shelf to hold everything from artwork and fresh flowers to magazines. Each side of the headboard contains generous recessed shelving, reclaiming space for books, extra blanket storage, and bedside essentials.
Pockets sewn onto a slipcovered ottoman, *right*, make it the perfect spot to change into slippers and begin to relax when the workday is done.

Storage can be as attractive as any other
element in a room. Use your ingenuity.
Well-chosen containers add visual interest.

Storage is arranged at every level in this bedroom for ease of use and graceful effect. Near the floor, baskets set within the framework of tables and shelves accentuate the room's natural palette. Along the wall, an inspired intermingling of antique and new storage creates a whimsical open closet, constructed from a Shaker-style peg rail and vertical white shelving towers. A sleek, frameless oval mirror keeps the look clean and modern.

A split-wood basket, *left*, nestled in a bamboo table, holds bedside necessities. **Recessed shelves**, *above*, hold audio equipment and create display space. **A Shaker-inspired peg rail and shelf**, *right*, hang above a portable canvas catchall box.

Design Details

Distributing storage all around a room helps integrate it with the space. As the furnishings in this bedroom demonstrate, varying the height of storage components spreads the visual impact throughout the room. Take advantage of perspective, too. Notice how both the shelves in the headboard and in the walls flanking the bed are out of sight when you enter the room. Give shelves a little breathing space by leaving areas around them open.

Simple and subtle, *left*, a stitched cotton pocket hangs neatly on the bed to keep glasses and reading material handy. The headboard marries style and function, with built-in side shelves and a top ledge for display. On the bed, ivory chenille and embroidered cotton velvet pillow covers are layered on snow-white sheets for a lush contrast of texture. **Tucked-under storage**, *above*, combines order and style.

Color Palette

In areas where you need a lot of storage and organization to help control clutter, it's a good idea to use a color palette that helps your cause. White is a smart choice because it reflects light and makes a room feel more spacious and clean. Here, a neutral scheme of creamy whites is set against a fresh background of the palest yellow. Accented with honeyed shades of light brown – in the seagrass rug, wood furniture, and wicker baskets – the palette makes the room feel natural and refreshing.

Materials

Seagrass This straw-like fiber comes from aquatic plants grown in many countries in South Asia. Its smooth surface and subtle green tone add warmth and an outdoors appeal to a room. The fiber's natural stain resistance also makes it ideal for rugs in high-traffic areas such as bedrooms.

Split-wood basket Basket weaving is one of the oldest art forms of human civilization. This strong, wide weave of wood slats yields a sturdy container reminiscent of classic Shaker picnic baskets. Wicker baskets are woven of bendable twigs or branches.

Chenille Aptly named after the French word for caterpillar, chenille fabric weaves silk or cotton into tufted cords for greater depth and richness. This luxuriously nubby material, commonly used in blankets and sweaters, calls out to be touched.

Customizing a Closet

Walk-in closets serve every storage need.
Create organization and clean symmetry with a
sleek white storage system, customized to hold
everything from jewelry to bed linens.

Simply put, a well-designed closet
can keep you organized. To plan and
create a dream closet, sort through
and select cabinet options (the
drawers and cupboards) and be clever
about the extras. Storage can be open,
or hidden inside drawers or behind
doors. A few flat, slide-out panels
among the drawers are handy; use
them for folding and sorting clothes.
Drawers should include dividers, and
hardware should operate effortlessly.
A wealth of mirrors doubles the
apparent size of the space.

A graduated bureau design, *left and right,*
has small drawers at the top for jewelry and
grooming supplies, and deeper ones below for
clothes. Mirrored doors conceal a luggage closet.
Brushed chrome hardware, *above,* is cylindrical
but notched for ease of grasping.

How to Organize Storage

A simple strategy for getting organized lies in just three words: categorize, consolidate, and contain. In the bedroom, categories are likely to be clothing, bedding, books, and vanity items. Each should have a dedicated container and a single location (to save time spent hunting for what you need). When selecting containers, keep in mind that the better a container suits what's stored, the more you'll use it. More creative thinking is needed for what's in full view than for accessories stowed in drawers and closets. Using whimsical containers for small items – wine crates, apothecary jars, or baskets, for example – helps keep your belongings neat and cleverly displayed at the same time.

Vintage suitcases, *top*, make handsome storage compartments. The handles let you move them easily. **Woven baskets**, *above*, slide right under benches, beds, and tables to make the most of limited space. **Grooming and vanity items**, *right*, can be put on display if you're short on space. Staying within a single color palette keeps them looking tidy.

Divide and conquer, *left*, with built-in shelving wherever possible. Categorize by season and keep only current needs on view. **A hideaway linen cabinet**, *below*, is concealed behind wainscoting. **Wine crates**, *bottom*, fit handily under the bed.

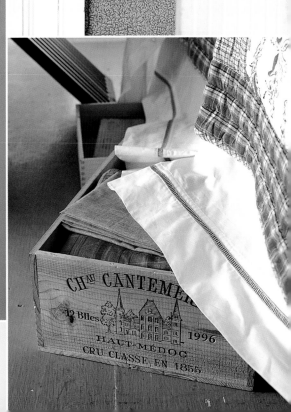

accessories

Design, it's often said, is in the details. Accessories are the details that bring a room to life, reflecting the personalities of the people who inhabit it. They can be treasured bits of family history (your grandmother's antique mirror, a bowl filled with pinecones collected on your honeymoon) or a store-bought bauble that caught your eye. They can be exquisitely simple objects from nature or the product of human ingenuity and artistry. Whatever form they take, accessories enrich and enliven a bedroom with vivid dashes of color and layers of meaning.

them with carpets and throws during winter. Have light, delicate accessories ready for spring: sheer voile curtains, crisp cotton bedding, or seagrass rugs to lighten a dark wood floor. In cooler weather, top sheers with a second layer of velvet curtains, and bring in fluffy down blankets or a faux-fur throw. Let the seasons be your guide.

The bed is a natural place to start when you're considering new accessories. No matter what the frame or headboard style, a bed gets much of its personality from the linens that dress it. Think opposites. Give the ornate lines of an iron bed

Accessories transform a bedroom. Don't be shy about changing or adding to them; they express your spirit in this room. Keep it lively. Have a little fun.

These details are the easiest elements to change in a room, and the best way to refresh an interior or to reinvent it completely. Use your imagination. The goal should be less planning, more creativity. Go with what you love – antique-fair treasures, mementos, souvenirs, pictures of places you've traveled to or ones that you dream about. Remember that accessories do more than decorate; they also can unify a room, tying together eclectic themes and creating an integrated space.

Changing accessories with the seasons can bring comfort and variety to a bedroom. Try the Southern approach of dressing rooms in cool linens and pale colors for summer, then layering

a crisp, tailored coverlet; update a traditional sleigh bed with a scattering of brilliantly colored silk pillows; layer vintage linens from different eras with fresh new ones. Most important, make sure your bed linens feel as good as they look.

Surfaces can be softened or enhanced with accessories. Bring new texture and color to tables and shelves with fresh flowers and botanicals. Drape a lamp shade with a beaded crystal necklace to add a note of glamour. Make the floor warmer and more inviting with chenille or wool rugs or richly textured kilims. You can never go wrong with accessories in the bedroom if you surround yourself with the things you love.

Mixing Memories

Eclectic bedrooms have stories to tell. They're spaces where the decor has evolved slowly, layer by layer, and the mix of objects old and new reads like a visual biography of their collector.

Arranging accessories of different materials, styles, and provenances takes thoughtful attention to detail. Find a common element like a color or a theme that relates eclectic accessories to the room and to each other.

In this bedroom, the artwork sets the boundaries for the color palette, which comes through in the strong hues of the bedding, the rug, and the gold dupioni silk drapes. Along with a use of bold color, a clever repetition of geometric shapes and graphic styles helps to unify the room's distinctive collection.

Vintage French posters for wine and caviar inspire the strong color choices of this bedroom. **A bronze lamp,** *this page,* with a glass mosaic shade sits atop an antique bank safe. **A chemist's beaker,** *far left,* is put to good use as a vase.

Keeping It Simple

In every great design, it's the little touches that make a room come alive. For small bedrooms, a few accessories are often enough; it's just a matter of choosing the perfect ones.

The most peaceful bedrooms are often the simplest. Just a few carefully chosen objects can infuse a compact space with tranquility and warmth. Keeping fabrics all white and displaying only one of each type of accessory – a solitary framed painting, a modest swing-arm lamp, a single clear glass vase – allows each element to stand out.

Accessories needn't be used in pairs, even if they were purchased that way. Dividing matching lamps between two rooms, for example, can help weave a consistent style throughout a home. Pairing objects may offer symmetry, but showcasing one alone highlights its uniqueness and sculptural qualities.

A headboard upholstered
in crisp linen, *opposite top*,
is a clean backdrop for a richly
textured matelassé pillow sham.
**Sheer café curtains edged
with lace**, *opposite right*, admit
light while ensuring privacy.
A clean palette, *this page,* is
warmed by flowers in a classic
Alvar Aalto glass vase.

A sleigh bed, *this page,* is dressed in faux suede, serape-stripe cotton pillows, and a quilted patchwork coverlet. A bandana-inspired blanket, *right,* used as a wall covering and a hand-embroidered pillow give a timeless look to this cozy reading corner. A denim-blue cabinet, *far right,* provides an unexpected splash of color.

Classic Comforts

Handcrafted accessories take center stage in simple surroundings. Make the most of a rustic backdrop by offsetting it with the warm presence of quilts, woven rugs, and vintage accents.

Handcrafted items have a durability and character that make a bedroom feel inviting and lived in. The timeless beauty of woven kilim rugs, piecework quilts, and vintage textiles lends a room a laid-back presence.

Textured and unadorned, this bedroom's pine-plank floors and rammed-earth walls make it the perfect setting for collectible heirloom accessories. From the well-worn stack of Pullman cases to the layered flat-weave dhurrie and kilim rugs, each element is arranged for casual comfort. Even the color palette is simple and unfussy: deep reds, rich browns, and classic blue suit a room in which relaxation is central.

A Bed for All Seasons

Because the bed is a bedroom's most prominent feature, a change of linens brings a fresh style with minimal effort. Furnish your bed with luxurious layers that can be changed, turned back, and rearranged. Think of your bedding as another option for stylish accessorizing that can be tailored to suit the seasons. With a simple swap-out of accents to complement the new look, the whole room seems to have been redone.

Wrap up in comfort, *opposite*, with faux suede and a faux-fur throw. Both are durable, luxurious, and, unlike the real thing, washable. **A floral satin-weave duvet**, *left*, and matching pillow shams celebrate spring. Tinted sheets are a colorful contrast when turned down. **Sumptuous silk**, *below left*, is a perfect all-season fabric. It's light and breathable, yet warm in winter. **Yarn-dyed cotton bedding**, *below*, has a light, cool texture that's a refreshing pleasure against the skin on summer nights.

How to Accessorize a Bedroom

Changing or rearranging accessories keeps a room lively and interesting. To be an accomplished accessorizer means being a browser, on the lookout for interesting goods and at the ready to change your room. Accessories need not be expensive; displays of found objects like leaves or beachcombing finds have timeless appeal. Try assigning goods a new role: use china dishes or large shells to hold jewelry, or recruit hat racks to organize handbags. Simple, beautiful ideas can be found anywhere.

Functional accessories, *above*, like this brightly striped laundry bag hanging from a mirror, add bold, individual style to a room in an instant. **Ordinary things can be extraordinary**, *right*, when put to imaginative use. A garden trellis and antique-china dishes are inspired ideas for providing storage with style.

Bring in the garden, *above*, with a convex mirror set low to reflect the view. Or, use fresh flowers as a colorful accessory that changes weekly. Soft and comfortable pillows, the ultimate bedroom accessory, are an easy way to add a touch of whimsy. Pillar candles set a mood for unwinding.

Painting a shelf with chalkboard paint, *above right*, is a stylish way to create a forum for inspirational thoughts or daily reminders. Paint effects such as faux satin or suede make everyday items decorative. **A whimsical grouping of favorite objects**, *right*, can provide an offbeat touch.

display

Arranged with care, an artistic display of objects is one of the most personal ways to decorate a bedroom. Displays focus attention on artwork, found treasures, and curios that hold special meaning, and they contribute to a room's character and mood as well as its style.

Displayed objects can suggest achievements, memories, or even humor. A bedroom collection is often more private than what's on display elsewhere in the house. You're free to choose things that make you smile as you drift off to sleep or ones that you love seeing when you first awake.

The arrangement of objects can say as much about a room as the things themselves. Extensive collections of similar items – old alarm clocks, vintage radios, record albums, or books – can be arranged easily on shelves because of their sheer volume and clear similarity. Smaller objects and disparate pieces can be more of a challenge.

Try grouping items that are alike in color, texture, or theme to make a collection appear cohesive. Almost anything can be elevated to the level of artwork if treated with respect in presentation and display. Three vases in varied shapes

The things on view in the bedroom express who you are. Thoughtfully chosen and carefully displayed, they reflect your individual experiences.

If you're fortunate enough to have a handsome painting to hang on the wall, by all means give it pride of place. But you don't need museum-quality artwork to create a beautiful bedroom. A themed grouping of photos (family, wedding, vacation), all in mismatched frames, could be a perfect complement to an eclectically dressed bed. Displayed with care, a quilt, a kilim, or an ordinary swath of lovely fabric used as a wall hanging can be just as appealing as an antique tapestry. Seashells, leaves, or twigs – even vintage signs or quirky old architectural mouldings – can be used to create distinctive displays. All it takes is imagination and confidence.

and sizes can look jumbled if their colors, styles, and textures are different as well. But if all three are McCoy pottery, Venetian glass, or cut crystal, or if all are bright red, the effect is striking.

Even functional items can be displayed with style. Take bedside necessities like a water glass and carafe and elevate them with a tealight votive and a vase of flowers, creating a grouping in clear glass. Once the art of display becomes second nature, you'll begin to look at your bedroom as a blank canvas just waiting to be filled with objects of beauty. The impulse to display reflects pride in the things you've chosen to keep. Show them off. They're a reflection of you.

A Collector's Bedroom

Rooms that are filled with collections are physical narratives of rich lives. Every corner is likely to contain a reminder of family, friends, and adventures. Thoughtful display lets each object speak for itself while striking a balance between spontaneity and symmetry.

Collectors' bedrooms tell you a lot about who lives there. Some people favor a simple room with a single area filled with display (perhaps a mantel or a picture wall); others want lots of favorite things all around the room. Whichever style you prefer, knowing the principles of color, scale, and placement can help you present your possessions creatively.

Art galleries have long used wall color as a way to pull together exhibits. Color can be painted on a single focal wall – perhaps where you'd like to place a group of pictures or hang display ledges – or it can be used all around a room to unify a range of dissimilar objects. Choosing a single color for picture frames or ledges also helps add visual unity. The practice of creating "steps" – grouping tall, medium, and low objects together – has also been employed for creating displays for centuries. Using scale in this way is helpful if the things you would like to display are different from one another but can be related by their height.

All these tricks are put to work in the bedroom shown here, where deep sienna walls frame a traveler's eclectic collection that includes shoemakers' forms, brass opera glasses, vintage clocks, cameras, and travel trunks.

A metal-and-wood ladder, *left*, is cleverly repurposed to hold mementos from all over the world, including a cigar box from Nicaragua and wooden shoemakers' forms. **A vintage globe**, *right*, sets the theme for this room at a glance: this is a world traveler's collection.

Shelves and ledges are great devices for display. Ledges don't require much wall space, and they can be used to arrange your own private gallery of themed prints, photographs, or favorite objects. To enliven a display on a shelf or ledge, try arranging objects by size or type, rather than simply lining them up in a row.

Display creates harmony: in an artful display of useful and beautiful collectibles, the sum becomes greater than the parts.

One simple idea for a well-composed room is a strategic placement of mirrors. In the eighteenth and nineteenth centuries, rooms with a fireplace always used over-mantel mirrors to emphasize space. In modern rooms, mirrors can also be used as a backdrop for collections, to accentuate objects. They multiply whatever is placed before them, so they seem to amplify a collection. Ordinarily, mirrors are hung with their center at eye level, but if their purpose is decorative, you may hang them at any height or even tip them slightly forward so they reflect a collection to advantage.

This space doesn't try too hard to show off its treasures. Instead, the sculptural qualities of the collections' pieces embellish the room's clean lines and create a cohesive decorative style.

Two silk lanterns play off the unifying background color. Twin lacquer-frame mirrors preside over an army trunk and folding writing desk used as nightstands; in the corner, a closed Victrola supports scrapbooks and a globe. At the desk, a leather-covered bistro-style chair is a chic choice that makes paperwork a pleasure.

In this bedroom, unexpected arrangements draw attention to displays. The spaces between the steps of a ladder, for instance, become a three-dimensional scrapbook, showing each item to advantage. Vertical arrangements work with scale in a provocative way; things that might have been overlooked are given presence.

The best displays share a hue, shape, or theme – or simply a taste for the quirky.

The rich colors of the walls, lamp shades, and floorboards serve as a unifying backdrop for the displays, and the repetition of black throughout the room brings consistency and order to the space. Furnishings chosen for their clean, classic lines add strength to the composition without drawing focus away from the displays of collectibles.

An old camera, *left*, on the mantel invites a closer look. Texture makes its way into the mix with leather, cowskin, raw linen, and soft faux fur, setting a warm tone for the collection. A display of traveler's finds, *right*, and a favorite photograph are reminders of voyages past and inspiration for exciting journeys to come.

Design Plan

Twin mirrors multiply the collections displayed on a desk and trunk.

Ledges present a dimensional display of clocks and cameras.

Black is a unifying element for multiple collections.

The mantel also serves as a display ledge for the collection.

The mirror, framed picture, and trunk create a geometric still-life.

A ladder becomes shelving for a stepped display arrangement.

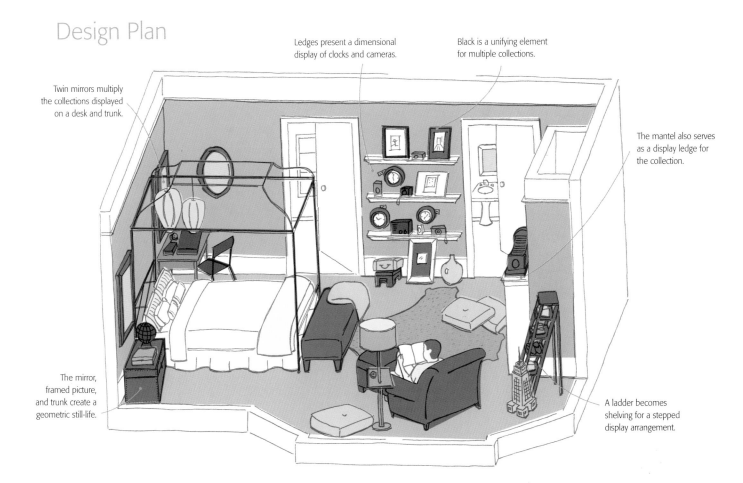

Color Palette

Sienna, an earth tone that originally took its hue from iron oxide, dominates the walls of this bedroom. Teamed with polished darks and lights, such as the stone fireplace and painted white trim, this bold color pops but doesn't lose its autumnal bent. Black accessories, chocolate-brown leather furniture, and brown floors contrast with the sienna, adding to this treasure-filled room's sophistication.

Room Plan

Collectibles and other treasured finds all seem at home in this display-rich room. For example, wall ledges house a quirky collection of old clocks and cameras. A cohesive feeling comes from a unifying display approach and the repetition of black and white against the deep sienna walls. The fireplace mantel and a step ladder offer more display space. The stepped levels flanking the bed – an old trunk on one side, a secretary on the other – offer ideas for how to display cherished items in unexpected ways.

Materials

Cowskin Animal skins make warm, soft rugs. Animal-print and faux-fur rugs can offer a similar graphic look.

Linen Made from the flax plant, linen has a textured, open weave that gives it lightweight breathability and a natural translucent quality.

Ticking This strong, tightly woven cotton, originally used to make mattresses, features a pattern of simple stripes against a natural background.

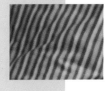

Displays That Work

Hardworking rooms need special consideration.
While a matched collection looks great almost
anywhere, the odds and ends of everyday life
require more adept arranging.

When a bedroom is used as a
multipurpose space, storage presents
a special challenge. A bedside table
need hold only necessities, but a desk
that also serves as a nightstand, like
the one in this home office/guest
room, must hold considerably more.

Often, the marriage of necessity
and creativity yields beautiful results.
Here, a homemade tackboard
provides an attractive storage solution;
it also creates an impromptu gallery
for displaying personal keepsakes.

A hardworking display, *left,* uses pulleys and
twine to keep a desktop organized. Yardsticks are
used as a border over grass cloth wallpaper to
create a tackboard. **A collection of glass vessels,**
above and right, makes a sculptural statement.

How to Arrange Bedroom Displays

Never underestimate the power of an eclectic arrangement. Bedrooms are a wonderful stage for displays of all kinds. The room's private nature invites the assembling of valued and treasured objects – perhaps too fragile to place in public rooms – and collections with the most personal meaning. Displays needn't be limited to walls; they can still make a statement in small or narrow spaces, such as windowsills, mantels, ledges, or picture rails. Interesting display techniques are as important as the objects themselves, so gather multiples, then arrange them to attract the eye. Don't overlook the element of surprise. Unexpected touches and clever ideas can add a twist that draws a smile.

Levels create a dynamic display, *above,* in this arrangement that mixes classic and modern sensibilities. Contrasts of old and new, polished and worn, add interest. **An assortment of frames,** *above right,* makes a lively display. Have fun with shapes and sizes to give texture to an arrangement; staying within a black-and-white palette brings cohesiveness to this grouping. **Collectible mercury glass,** *right,* anchors an arrangement that limits itself to silver and black for unity.

Family pictures don't need to be in frames, *above*. They'll attract more attention if they're informally attached with clothespins or paper clips to a ribbon or a branch. **A stepped arrangement**, *right*, is an elegant choice for a narrow wall. Collect paintings from flea markets in a variety of sizes and leave some unframed.

Room Resources

At Pottery Barn, we believe that casual, relaxed style is something you can weave through every space in your home, from front room to bedroom. For this book, we scoured hundreds of locations to find the perfect settings to create these special rooms. We experimented with colors, furnishings, rugs, drapes, and accessories to find the best combinations for each space. The results? This collection of style ideas, which we hope will inspire and delight you.

Each location chosen for this book was unique, and each delightful in its own way. Here is a little bit more about the homes we visited, the style ideas we created, and the individual elements that make each design tick.

A note about color: wherever possible in this list of resources, we've offered the actual paint manufacturer and paint color that was used in the room shown. We also list the closest Benjamin Moore paint color match (in parentheses) for each room. Because photography and color printing processes can dramatically change the way colors appear, it is very important to test swatches of any paint color you are considering in your own home where you can see how the light affects them at different times of the day.

Basics of Bedroom Style

This shingled hillside guest cottage and a slightly larger main cottage have small footprints that allow the beauty of the surroundings to star. The bedroom overlooks a vineyard.

Space Built in 1940 from mail-order, pre-fab kits, the 600-square-foot guest-house and the 850-square-foot main house were remodeled in 1998.

Color Walls, trim, and ceiling Benjamin Moore Swiss Coffee OC-45 satin.

Furnishings PB Basic hemstitch sheets, duvet, and shams; faux-fur throw and pillow shams; charcoal chenille throw; Metropolitan leather chairs and ottoman; solid voile drapes; colorbound seagrass rug; and PB Basic white towels, all from Pottery Barn. King bed with button-tufted leather headboard, tortoise-finish rattan and bamboo side table and bureau, primitive bench from New Mexico, ship's prism (on mantel).

Lighting Built-in overhead lighting. Vintage alabaster-base table lamps with silk shades. Antique iron-scroll floor lamp with Pottery Barn accordion shade.

Display Paris print, gallery frame, and chalkboard wall shelf, all from Pottery Barn. Photo of olives (on mantel) by Jeffrey Gibson. Salvaged architectural pediment (above bed).

pages 14–21

A Backyard Bedroom

Several guest tents like this one dot a mountainside property with a main house and a communal long-house with a kitchen, fireplace, patio, pool, and outdoor showers.

Space The tent rests on a permanent 13' 5" x 11' 3" wooden platform that includes a small entry porch. It has electricity and operable wood-framed windows. The interior's exposed wood structure provides ledges for storage and display. To buy a similar tent, contact Sweetwater Bungalows (800/587-5054; www.sweetwaterbungalows.com).

Color Painted plywood floors (Benjamin Moore Province Blue 2135-40 semi-gloss).

Furnishings Plantation patchwork quilt, Kauai plaid sheet set, jeweled organdy canopy, X table, wall cubbies, and camp lanterns, all from Pottery Barn. Vintage iron twin bed, secretary, and Adirondack-style table and stool. Antique iron-lashed wooden chest. Vanity area: treen shaving mirror, 1950s gilded-back mirror panel, galvanized marine lantern, English ironstone platter, and Italian ceramic pitcher. Florist's bucket as wastebasket.

Lighting Bedside industrial pendants.

Display Red hand-painted "steak dinners" sign from flea market.

pages 26–33

A Family-Friendly Bedroom

Part of a classic California crafts-man cottage, this contemporary bedroom is en suite with a bath. Zones for kids and adults fit in just 252 square feet of floor space.

Space To make the most of light and help conserve energy, windows are only on the front wall. A skylight illuminates the bath. Floors are pickled pine.

Color Lower walls and trim (Benjamin Moore White Opulence, OC-69 semi-gloss). Upper walls (Benjamin Moore Iced Mint 2030-70 flat). Floors Benjamin Moore Iced Mint 2030-70 over Alpine White 2147-70, thinned, applied, and sanded to show layers.

Furnishings Weathered wood bed, box-pleat bed skirt, white flannel sheets, Sutton bookcase, Nantucket mirror (on vanity), upholstered beanbag cube, chaise with twill slipcover, rolling storage basket, and checkerboard rug, all from Pottery Barn. Step stool and tabletop easel from Pottery Barn Kids. Custom-made blue denim duvet cover and shams, vintage cotton chenille throw, and antique handmade quilt pillows.

Lighting Recessed ceiling lighting. Fairmont lamp from Pottery Barn.

Display Pottery Barn Lydia frames with portraits by Gina Risso Photography.

pages 36–41

A Serene Sanctuary

In a seaside village, this upstairs bedroom in a two-story house overlooks a large formal garden and stately topiary hedges. A guest house and pool are also on-site.

Space En suite with a bath, this room has cathedral ceilings with exposed beams. Pairs of recessed storage cup-boards (hidden behind the wainscoting and operated by pressure latches) flank the bed. Architecture by Lee Mindel, Shelton, Mindel & Associates. Interior design by Martin Johnson, MJ Decorative Interiors (altered for Pottery Barn photo shoot). The floors are pickled hardwood.

Color Walls (Benjamin Moore Summer Shower 2135-60 flat white). Trim (Benjamin Moore Distant Gray OC-68 semigloss).

Furnishings Chambray cotton quilt and sheet set, white hemstitch pillowcases, channel-stitch silk shams, chenille throw, matelassé bed skirt, fringed denim pillow cover, Charlotte quilt, Mercer medicine cabinet, Maxime terry cubes, Cottage hamper stool and mini-vanity, and cedar chest, all from Pottery Barn. King head-board with cast-iron bird ornaments.

Lighting Overhead lighting, with Pottery Barn Halophane sconces.

Display Oil paintings from flea markets.

pages 50–55

Getting White Right

This hillside estate includes guest cottages, a gazebo, and a poolside cottage. Gardens surrounding the main house overlook mountains and a picturesque monastery.

Space This 17' x 21' bedroom has a cathedral ceiling with exposed beams. The wall and ceiling paneling is painted knotty pine barn board. The architecture echoes the loftiness of a barn.

Color Walls and ceilings Fuller O'Brien White Wing flat (Benjamin Moore White Heron, OC-57).

Furnishings Elena matelassé coverlet and shams, PB Basic hemstitch bed skirt, faux-fur throw and pillow, Sophia shelf, wicker and leather hamper, woven wood baskets, and wall-mounted conservatory lanterns, all from Pottery Barn. Custom queen bed with muslin headboard. Raw silk and natural linen shawls used as wall hangings. Yew wood occasional table. Nutura diamond jacquard-woven coir rug by Stark. Window seat cushions in striped linen from Chelsea Edwards. Custom-upholstered chairs in ribbed cot-ton. Henry Calvin off-white linen drapes.

Lighting Recessed overhead lighting with apothecary floor lamp; brushed nickel swing-arm lamps at window seats.

Display Photos by Andrea Gentl.

pages 68–75

Timeless Texture

This bedroom is tucked under the eaves of a two-story clapboard farmhouse located on a peaceful woodland road. In the summer, wildflowers surround the house.

Space At the top of a narrow stairway, this attic bedroom has lots of alcoves (one serves as a dressing area) and an adjoining octagonal bathroom. Instead of plaster, the ceilings are finished in narrow painted wood boards. Floors are wide white-painted barn board. Opposite the bed, recessed storage cupboards are hidden behind the paneling.

Color Walls and trim (Benjamin Moore Moonlight White 2143-60 satin).

Furnishings Elena matelassé coverlet, PB Basic hemstitch sheets, Stefano dining chair, and double-braided chenille rug, all from Pottery Barn. Antique iron bed. Custom white organdy headboard cover, taffeta bed skirt, and throw pillow. Raw silk accent pillow. Matched vintage carved-wood bureaus. Vintage cane-back chair and wrought-iron table. Striped silk gauze curtain panels (tacked directly to the window frame). McCoy pottery.

Lighting Vintage marble-base column lamps.

Display Oil paintings from flea markets.

pages 76–81

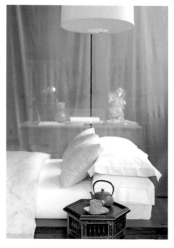

A Simple Change of Style

The master bedroom suite in this modernized saltbox cottage has skylights, French doors at each end, views of acres of salt marsh, and custom-built, floor-to-ceiling storage cabinets.

Space The room is 16' 6" x 14' 6" (not including the alcove) with a 10' ceiling and 2¼" knotty pine-plank floors. Architecture by Richard Martino and Will Schulz, Southampton, NY.

Color Walls (Benjamin Moore Atrium White, Interior Ready Mixed 79 flat); semigloss on ledges.

Furnishings PB Basic hemstitch sheets, French knot silk pillow, chenille throw, cherry leather Manhattan armchair, and X table, all from Pottery Barn. Oxidized iron queen sleigh bed. Custom table cover; custom red toile and gingham-check shams and bolsters. Homespun linen bolster with grosgrain ribbon ties. Vintage wooden linotype cabinet. Cotton canvas chairs by Jean Michel Frank.

Lighting Seventeenth-century English candlestick lamps; accordion-pleat shades from Pottery Barn. Pottery Barn tripod lamp. Recessed ceiling lighting.

Display *Ravello,* 1986, by Sally Gall, 20" x 24" silverprint, edition of 20. *Open Door* canvas from Pottery Barn.

Pages 88–95

Furnishing a Guest Room

This cottage, a converted carport, retains its original concrete floor. Part of a country estate, the cottage and two-story main house are on a steep hillside; they were completely redesigned in the late 1990s.

Space The homeowner, a furniture designer, has filled the cottage and main house with custom-made furniture, antiques, and Italian art. Interior walls are finished in rough, painted planks, as are the doors, for a seamless look.

Color Interior finishes are "rough painted" (Benjamin Moore Cotton Balls 2145-70) to allow underlying wood surfaces to show through.

Furnishings Linden iron daybed, ticking stripe bed skirt and sheets, Tulianne embroidered duvet cover and shams, Aris pedestal table, Augusta wicker chair, gingham nesting hatboxes, Americana coatrack, ivory wool shag rug, and linen drapes, all from Pottery Barn. Antique quilt accent pillow. Antique quilt on wall. Marble-topped Victorian commode. Reproduction transferware teapot.

Lighting The original ceiling with recessed can lights was removed to show off the beamed architecture. Now, table lamps and natural light illuminate this guest bedroom and home office.

Pages 96–103

Creating Drama with Light

The architecture of this twelve-year-old John Marsh Davis house was inspired by both traditional Japanese houses and the designs of Frank Lloyd Wright. The rooms welcome indoor play.

Space A 2,800-square-foot main house shares the property with a guest cottage, an artist's studio, and a playhouse. Walls are old-growth redwood, harvested from naturally fallen trees or recycled wood. Ceiling is fir. Floors are narrow-board oak. Doors by Davenport Mill, Santa Cruz, CA.

Color Walls (Benjamin Moore Raspberry Parfait 2172-40 satin).

Furnishings Tristan platform bed, Fiona coverlet and shams, PB Basic ottoman with twill slipcover, Stafford Bench, loop jute rug, leather pillows, camp lanterns, and pillar candles, all from Pottery Barn. Silk shibori accent pillow, Moroccan side tables, ribbed cream wool throw layered with silk Balinese sarong on chaise. Custom-made kilim floor pillow.

Lighting Pottery Barn nickel apothecary table lamp. Pendant lamp with crinkle paper shade, glass pillar bookcase lights, antique wrought-iron candle chandelier, and 1960s desk lamp with music stand base, grommeted vinyl shade.

Display All paintings by Karen Barbour.

Pages 112–19

Lighting for Ambience

This Victorian townhouse has five bedrooms and 12' ceilings. The all-white guest room decor is inspired by the homeowner's given name (which means "celestial") and is designed to seem as soft as a cloud.

Space This eclectically furnished dwelling has vintage mouldings and tall, nearly floor-to-ceiling windows, which set the stage for a romantic decor that plays with light and inspires dreams and relaxation.

Color Walls (Benjamin Moore Chantilly Lace 2121-70 flat).

Furnishings Whitney iron headboard, Elena matelassé coverlet and shams, and faux-chinchilla throw, all from Pottery Barn. Caroline jacquard sheets from Chambers. Belgian linen bed drapes. Marble-top French pastry table. Raw-edge gauze panel drapes. Antique chair frame with organza slipcover.

Lighting Crystal tier chandelier from Pottery Barn. Cylinder floor lamp draped with Bob Mackie white silk kimono-sleeve jacket with crystal, white matte jet, and silver beads. Hand-blown glass candle lamps. Bedside chandelier from the globe of a larger chandelier.

Pages 120–21

A Place for Everything

Custom-designed and built for a family, this master bedroom, en suite with a large bath, overlooks a backyard garden and tree-lined street. The bed alcove has recessed shelving in the bedside walls.

Space High ceilings, a natural color palette, architectural window treatments, and plenty of natural light help keep this bedroom feeling uncluttered and spacious. Architecture by Moller Willrich Architecture, San Francisco, CA.

Color Walls (Benjamin Moore Greenmount Silk HC-3 flat).

Furnishings Autumn garden coverlet and shams, white chenille duvet and shams, PB Basic hemstitch sheets, woven wood storage baskets, Santa Fe storage basket, frameless oval mirror, Thomas dresser, Tibetan console table, Stafford bar stool, and PB Basic ottoman and Megan chair with twill slipcovers, all from Pottery Barn. Custom-designed white twill pockets beside bed and on ottoman. Tortoise bamboo bedside table. Amish Arts Shaker components used to create storage area.

Lighting Built-in recessed lighting. Vintage glass-base bedside lamp.

Display Abstract oil and charcoal on canvas by Susan Spies.

Pages 142–47

Mixing Memories

Vintage finds fill this sophisticated bedroom in a country ranch home. Raw pine floorboards and exposed-beam architecture are the perfect foils for rich materials and a bold collection of artwork.

Space Four sets of French doors open the room to the outdoors. The bedroom overlooks a barn, stables, and a backyard with a spreading shade tree.

Color Walls and ceiling (Benjamin Moore Pure White OC-64 flat).

Furnishings PB Basic hemstitch sheet set, chenille throw, reversible silk quilt, channel-stitch silk red pillow sham, kilim rug, dupioni silk drapes, and adjustable wrought-iron rods, all from Pottery Barn. Burgundy velvet and red pinch-stitch velvet accent pillows. Vintage bank safe and wrought-iron bench.

Lighting Vintage bronze pedestal base table lamp with amber glass mosaic shade.

Display Vintage French advertising posters courtesy of Sarah Stocking Fine Vintage Posters, San Francisco, CA. Chemist's glass beaker in stand used as a vase.

Pages 156–57

Classic Comforts

This rammed-earth house was crafted with centuries-old building techniques. The homeowner specializes in rammed-earth construction and created this home in 1999 to showcase his work.

Space On the second floor of this 2,600-square-foot, two-story house, this bedroom overlooks a formal courtyard garden. Inspired by a farmhouse the homeowners admired in the Rhone Valley of France, the house has thick walls and deep recesses at the windows and doors. Rammed-earth buildings don't rely on precise "hard" angles, so walls can be easily patched with grout or grout-washed to emphasize or hide flaws. The floor is terra tile: unpainted, sealed, and waxed 1½"-thick cast earth.

Color Natural ginger wall and floor color from rammed earth. Wardrobe is painted Ralph Lauren Hacienda blue.

Furnishings Valencia double bed, crazy quilt coverlet, hemstitch sheets, Mesa everydaysuede™ duvet cover and pillow shams, and Sullivan leather ottoman, all from Pottery Barn. Vintage Pullman cases and hatbox. Stickley-style rocker.

Display *Barn* and *Fence,* Western photography series from Pottery Barn.

Pages 160–61

A Collector's Bedroom

Designed as a private haven for a world traveler, this second-story bedroom features city views, Victorian architecture, and an adjoining study. A display wall acts as a three-dimensional scrapbook.

Space The high ceilings, nearly floor-to-ceiling windows, a generous fireplace, and wraparound picture rails are features typical of Victorian architecture.

Color Walls (Benjamin Moore Rust 2175-30 satin). Trim (Benjamin Moore White Opulence OC-69 semigloss).

Furnishings PB Basic hemstitch sheets and bed skirt, Sierra stripe pillows, wrought-iron adjustable curtain rods, crown moulding ledges, Metropolitan leather chair and ottoman, and Sutton ladder bookcase, all from Pottery Barn. Metal canopy bed. Bedside vintage army trunk with portable Victrola, scrapbooks, and globe. Folding desk with bistro chair.

Display Camera collection, bottom ledge (left to right): wooden movie camera, Revere 8mm movie camera, Argus camera, Argoflex 75 camera (hanging), and Yashica 8mm camera; middle: vintage movie camera and Bell & Howell movie camera; top: vintage camera and crystal mini-camera. Photos by Michal Venera.

Pages 170–77

Glossary

Aalto, Alvar Considered one of the foremost architects and designers of the twentieth century, the Finnish architect and furniture designer Alvar Aalto, (1898–1976) worked collaboratively with his wife, Aino Marsio (1894–1949), a distinguished furniture designer in her own right. Many of his stylish, classic designs for laminated furniture are still in production today.

Adirondack During the late nineteenth and early twentieth centuries, the Adirondack Park in northeast New York became a vacation spot for wealthy families. They furnished their retreats using local materials, giving rise to the term Adirondack camp style. Typically, Adirondack furniture is rustic, hand-crafted, and uses every part of the tree. Vintage furnishings and accessories are considered collectible, and modern versions of this style are being made today.

Beadboard The most common type of wainscoting, beadboard gets its name from the regularly spaced bumps that are milled along the length of each piece. This form of wainscoting became widely available with the advent of industrial milling in the 1850s and was a popular feature of Victorian homes. It can be used on walls or as a colorfully painted headboard or bookcase detailing to add nostalgic charm to a bedroom.

Biedermeier This term refers to a style of furniture, decoration, and art popular in Germany in the early to mid-nineteenth century. Adapted from French Empire style, Biedermeier furnishings were simpler in design and emphasized comfort and affordability of materials, such as the use of black-lacquer bands in place of ebony inlays.

Bolster This term refers to a type of pillow or cushion that is long and narrow.

Canvas This durable fabric is commonly used for sporting goods, awnings, and outdoor furnishings. When used for drapes, slipcovers, or pillows, it brings a casual feel to a room. Canvas can be made from linen, hemp, or cotton and is available bleached, unbleached, or in a variety of dyed hues.

Cement A term often used interchangeably with concrete, cement is actually the fine gray powder that is mixed with water, sand, and gravel to make concrete. It is also used to make stucco, plaster, mortar, and grout.

Chenille Aptly named after the French word for caterpillar, chenille fabric weaves silk or cotton into tufted cords for great depth and richness. This luxuriously nubby material is commonly used to make blankets and sweaters. A soft chenille throw adds a cozy touch to a bed, while chenille drapes give a bedroom a plush feeling of warmth.

Chiffon This lightweight, sheer fabric can be made of silk or rayon. It is often used to make decorative ribbons and laces.

Coir This natural fiber is derived from the husks of coconuts, grown in Sri Lanka and other tropical locations. Once removed from the husks, the fiber is spun and machine-woven into matting, and often backed with latex for increased durability. A popular floor covering, coir is tough, resilient, and more textural than other natural-fiber rugs. It is exceptionally durable, which makes it an excellent choice in high-traffic areas. The color of coir varies based on its harvest time.

Concrete Cement, sand, water, and gravel form this strong, easy-to-maintain material. Recent innovations in dyeing and tinting allow concrete to be made in any color and even etched with designs. No longer relegated just to roads, driveways, and curbs, concrete is now being used to create interior flooring, fireplace surrounds, kitchen and bath countertops, and furniture. Decorative finishes include acid etching, stamping, polishing, staining, and painting.

Cotton twill Twill fabrics are characterized by a raised diagonal design and are noted for their firm, close weave. Denim is an example of cotton twill.

Denim Originally thought to be from France, this durable cotton fabric became popular in the United States during the California Gold Rush, in the form of work pants (jeans). It is also a great washable slipcover option for casual bedrooms, especially where kids and pets play. Repeated washings will soften the fabric and fade the traditional indigo color, adding to its appeal. White denim can be used for a more sophisticated look.

Dhurrie This flat-weave rug is traditionally made of colored cotton (but now is also seen in wool) and loomed in geometric designs. The style originated in India.

Dupioni silk Woven from two threads of the same or different colors, dupioni silk shimmers and seems to change color in the light. The fabric is woven from an irregular, rough silk thread that is the result of two silkworms spinning the same cocoon. It has textural bumps, or "slubs," similar to those of raw silk.

Faux fur This plush material is synthetic and as soft and warm as the real thing. Not just for coats and jackets, faux fur is used to make bedspreads, pillow covers, and throws.

Faux suede Designed to mimic the look and touch of genuine napped leather, this durable synthetic is luxurious to the eye and hand. Made of microfibers, it offers a soft, washable upholstery option for sofas and chairs, and it contributes a soft, lush feeling to rooms.

Fieldstone Rough-hewn stone, found in fields where the bedrock is close to the surface, fieldstone links a home to its natural surroundings. Stone in its natural form has a rustic quality. In contrast, quarry-cut stone is smoother and more regularly shaped.

Flat weave Created on a loom, a flat-weave rug is smoothly finished with no knots or pile, like a tapestry. A wool flat-weave rug such as a kilim is often reversible and makes a durable floor covering for high-traffic areas.

French doors Also called French windows, these originated in France during the late Renaissance. Generally hung in pairs, French doors swing open on hinges and have divided glass panels. They are commonly used to connect a house to a garden but are also popular inside the home wherever doors are needed but light is desirable.

Gingham This lightweight cotton fabric seems like the very definition of Americana, but in fact it originally came from India. The classic red-and-white checkerboard pattern was an American enhancement.

Glass Generally made of minerals called silicates, glass describes a type of material with a liquid-like molecular structure that, when melted and cooled, becomes rigid without crystallizing. While clear and colored glass allow light to shine through, other effects are also possible. Sand-blasted glass has a cooler, frosted look, while a semi-opaque glass diffuses light without fully blocking it.

Hemstitching This decorative sewing technique refers to a row of openwork stitching that defines the hemline edge of a garment or linen. It is traditionally seen in bed linens and table linens and may be done by hand or machine.

Jute A strong, woody plant fiber grown extensively in Asia, jute is noted for its innate strength and longevity. When woven, it has a lush, wool-like texture and appearance. Soft and durable, jute rugs work well in high-traffic areas.

Kilims These flat-weave and often reversible wool rugs are similar to dhurries but generally have bolder, more intricate designs. Originally designed to be placed on sandy desert floors by nomadic peoples of countries such as Iran, Iraq, Pakistan, and Turkey, kilim rug patterns represent different tribes and regions. All are rich, vibrant, and geometric, and they complement contemporary interiors.

Leather Tanned animal hides make a durable upholstery option that gets softer and more beautiful with use. The dimensions, surface texture, softness, and pigment regularity of the hide all distinguish high-quality leather. Black and brown are classic leather colors, but manufacturers now dye leathers in a range of hues. When dyed a bright yellow or cherry red, leather takes on a contemporary look.

Linen Woven from the fibers of the flax plant, linen is possibly the first fabric produced by humans. It can be as fine and sheer as a handkerchief or as substantial as canvas. Twice as strong as cotton, linen softens with washing. This versatile fabric is commonly used for bedding and upholstery. Lightweight linen curtains provide privacy while still allowing sunlight to shine through. Vintage pieces can contribute a sense of history to a room's decor.

Matelassé This handsome double-woven fabric, named for the French word for "quilted," has raised decorative patterns on its surface that mimic the look of a quilt. The effect is achieved through the process of weaving in an interlocking wadding weft (a filling thread or yarn), rather than through quilting. A matelassé bedspread will become softer with repeated washings and adds warm texture wherever it is used.

McCoy pottery The Nelson McCoy Sanitary Stoneware Company (later renamed the Nelson McCoy Pottery Company) was established in 1910 in Roseville, Ohio, for the production of functional and decorative stoneware. Until closing its doors in 1990, the company expanded its line of products, turning out specialty art pottery decorated with leaf and berry motifs; planters shaped like animals; cookie jars; and a line of dinnerware. Today, McCoy pottery is a popular collectible.

Mercury glass Developed in England in the 1840s, mercury glass (also called silvered glass) is a double-walled glass that contains a coating of silver nitrate, giving it the appearance of silver. Today it is highly collectible.

Mirrors The most common type of mirror is made of plate glass that has been coated on one side with metal or some other reflective surface. With their curved surfaces, convex and concave mirrors can add an element of fun or mystery. Mirrors can make a bedroom look bigger and can amplify its light. Unusual, antique, or wooden frames add style.

Natural fibers Rugs and pillow coverings made of natural fibers such as hemp, pandan grass, seagrass, jute, sisal, and coir add texture, warmth, and visual interest to a bedroom.

Organdy This stiff, transparent fabric made of cotton or silk is commonly used for making curtains. It is available with patterns or in solid colors.

Pickled wood The decorative technique called pickling describes a whitewashing effect that makes pine and other woods look pale and bleached with age.

Pine This wood from coniferous trees (which produce cones) tends to be softer than wood from deciduous trees (which shed leaves). Still, it is a popular choice for furniture, flooring, and cabinetry because of its rustic quality. Old pine is best for floors. Another option is a harder species such as white pine, a straight-grained wood with little resin that is often used for interior trim as well.

Quilt Patchwork may have been born of a necessity to recycle scraps of fabric, but sewing together different fabrics soon became an American art form predominantly practiced by women, and a traditional gift of love and remembrance. The top of a patchwork quilt is sewn from scraps or blocks of fabric generally selected for their complementary colors or graphic pattern. A whole-cloth quilt is a solid piece of fabric, which shows off intricate stitchery. A colorful quilt gives a bedroom an instant sense of tradition.

Raw silk Fabric or yarn made from untreated silk has a nubby feel and a low sheen. Raw silk's durability and gentle drape make it a good choice for curtains.

Seagrass Commercially grown in China, seagrass produces a fiber that is similar to straw and smoother than coir, sisal, or jute. Its smooth surface and subtle green tone add warmth and an outdoors appeal to the bedroom. The fiber's rugged durability also makes seagrass rugs suitable for high-traffic areas.

Shag rug A soft, deep pile makes shag rugs a comfy underfoot option for a bedroom with a casual style.

Shaker style This term refers to the simple, functional, and unornamented style that characterizes the finely crafted furnishings and handcrafts produced by the Shakers (formally known as the United Society of Believers), a religious group established in the early nineteenth century in New Lebanon, New York. Today, Shaker style continues to shape design sensibilities, and vintage Shaker furnishings are considered highly collectible.

Shibori silk A process of hand-dyeing silk by controlling the dye flow through folds sewn into the fabric, this Japanese fabric art is often likened to tie-dyeing. Shibori, however, requires greater precision because silk is so absorbent.

Sisal This flexible fiber is made from the leaves of the sisal (or agave) plant, which grows in Africa and Central America. Softer to the touch than coir but still durable, sisal is commonly woven into flat rugs with an even, highly textural surface. Sisal rugs hide dirt, resist stains, and absorb sounds, making them practical in high-traffic areas.

Split-wood basket Basket weaving is one of the oldest art forms of human civilization. A strong, wide weave of wood slats yields a sturdy container reminiscent of classic Shaker picnic baskets. Wicker baskets are woven of bendable twigs or branches.

Taffeta A crisp, smooth, plain-woven silk or linen fabric, taffeta is distinguished by its lustrous sheen. Although traditionally used for ball gowns and formal women's fashions, it's also an ideal choice for window treatments and bed skirts.

Ticking Originally used primarily to make mattress and pillow coverings, this strong, tightly woven cotton fabric features a characteristic pattern of simple stripes against a natural background. Today the term describes a variety of striped fabrics that have many uses in the home, from bed linens to curtains.

Treen From Middle English meaning "of the tree," treen or treenware most often describes wooden cookware, tableware, or eating utensils. It can also refer to wooden items with domestic, personal, or professional utility, such as a mirror.

Trundle A lower bed that slides or rolls out from beneath a standard bed, a trundle bed is popular for children and their sleepover guests. Many trundles can be raised up to match the level of the original beds, effectively turning a twin bed into a double to sleep adult guests.

Turned legs/posts Turning is the process by which cylindrical pieces of wood, such as furniture legs and posts, are carved in symmetrical patterns. Sharp tools are held against the wood as it spins on a lathe to create grooves and contours.

Twill This smooth, durable fabric is tightly woven, usually of cotton, and has a raised diagonal grain. Washable and relatively flat, this versatile weave is a good choice for slipcovers or upholstery in both summer and winter seasons. Denim and gabardine are examples of twill weaves. Brushed twill is finished to emphasize the fabric's soft nap.

Venetian mirrors With hand-beveled edges and delicate floral etching, this distinctive style of ornate, handcrafted mirror is a specialty of Venice that dates back to the Renaissance.

Venetian glass The city of Venice has been a world-renowned center of glassmaking since the Middle Ages. Specialties include transparent and delicate *cristallo* glass, which is blown into intricate designs; thinly sliced, colorful *millefiori* canes; and *lattimo,* or milk glass, an opaque white glass used to make elaborate patterns in clear glass. From a simple, delicate vase to the most elaborate curving chandelier, this fine glassware adds beauty to the home.

Voile This lightweight, soft fabric is traditionally made from cotton or silk, but can also be made of wool or synthetic fibers. Light plays off its sheerness, so voile curtains make a bedroom feel light-infused but not sunbaked.

Wainscoting Originally developed to prevent wall damage in heavy-traffic areas, *wainscoting* usually refers to wooden boards or panels that cover the lower portion of a wall. The term can also refer to full-height wall paneling. Beadboard, which has a regular raised pattern on the wood, is the most common type of wainscoting.

Wicker Created by weaving flexible branches or twigs from plants such as bamboo, cane, rattan, reed, or willow around a coarser frame, wicker is commonly used to make durable baskets and furniture. Wicker baskets and hampers offer an attractive storage solution in the bedroom. A durable material, wicker can stand up to a century of normal use.

Wrought iron Iron bar stock is forged or bent into shape to create decorative and architectural elements such as bed frames, grates, wine racks, and balcony and stair railings. Decorative forms include Gothic tracery, plant forms, and classical motifs. Today, wrought iron is sometimes actually made of steel.

Index

Acknowledgments

Contributing Editor
Martha Fay

Project Editor
Laurie Wertz

Copy Editors
Kristine Carber
Elizabeth Dougherty
Francine Hornberger

Designer
Jackie Mancuso

Illustrators
Robert Evans
Paul Jamtgaard
Nate Padavick

Indexer
Ken DellaPenta

Photography Assistants
Bill Moran
Hudson Cuneo
Paul Delehanty

Stylist Assistants
Greg Lowe
Curtis Speer
Joshua Young

Lead Merchandise Coordinator
Joshua Young

Merchandise Coordinators
Max Baloian
Matt Blankenzee
L. A. Daniels
Catherine Dill
C. J. Rosseler
Roger Smoothy
Joey Tosi

Weldon Owen thanks the photography and editorial teams for their creativity and stamina in producing this book and acknowledges the following people and organizations for their invaluable contribution in:

Allowing us to photograph their wonderful homes
Howard & Lori Backen, Karen Barbour & David Sheff, Mark & Tami Becker, Catherine Chermayeff, David Easton & Cynthia Wright, Jeffrey Gibson & Neal Ward, Robert & Kelli Glazier, Sam & Diana Hunt, Joanne Loube, Richard Martino, Leslie Murdock, Timothy O'Brien, Rod Rougelot, Tom & Linda Scheibal, Jon Staub, Celia Tejada, and Stephen & Kelly Willrich

Supplying artworks or props
Karen Barbour, Kevin Crandall, Sally Gall, Andrea Gentl, Jeffrey Gibson, David Lujan, Joan O'Connor (Timeless Treasures), Gina Risso Photography, Susan Spies, Sarah Stocking Fine Vintage Posters, Celia Tejada, and Michal Venera

Catering on location
Food & Company, Edie Goettler (Edie's Catering), The Golden Pear Café, Kass Kapsiak (Catering by Kass), Chris Ludwick (Grape Vine Catering Company), Jesse A. Rivas, and Spoon Catering

Providing assistance, advice, or support
Allison Arieff, Jim Baldwin, Monica Bhargava, Emma Boys, Garrett Burdick, Gregory D. Cann, Noël Casiano, Anne Crary, Val Cipollone, Joseph De Leo, Marti Emmons, Christie Every, Holly Harrison, Tom Hassett, Catherine Hill, Sam Hoffman (New Lab), Anjana Kacker, Katherine L. Kaiser, Bob Kapoor (Duggal Color Projects), Steve Knowlden, Susan Kokot-Stokes, Randall Koll, Holly Li, Charlene Lowe, Jennifer Martin, Dung Ngo, Emily Noh, Joan Olson, Pottery Barn Creative Services, Patrick Printy, Andrea Raisfeld, Philip Rossetti, Cynthia Rubin, Peter Scott, Karen Shapiro, Amy Shebes, Anthony Spurlock, Jason Stewart, Kelly Tagore, Esther Tamondong, Sara Terrien, Juli Vendzules, The Village Latch Inn, and Dena Zemsky

Author Acknowledgment
I would like to thank editor extraordinaire Shawna Mullen for expertly finessing my text, constantly keeping me on track, and tireless cheerleading.

All photography by Prue Ruscoe and styling by Edward Peterson, except for:
Jacket front flap, photography by Christina Schmidhofer © 2003. Materials swatches in Design Details and Find Your Style, pages 34–35, 180 (center), photography by Dan Clark. Pages 62 (top), 124 (bottom), photography by Dan Clark and styling by Laura Guido-Clark. Pages 122 (left), 124 (top), 165 (left), photography by Alan Williams and styling by Michael Walters. Page 135, photography by Michal Venera. Pages 4–5, 24, 60 (top), 61 (top and right), 122 (right), 123 (left), 154, styling by Helen Crowther.

About Pottery Barn

Founded in 1949 as a single store in Manhattan, Pottery Barn has evolved into America's leading source for style. For more than fifty years, Pottery Barn has brought comfort, style, and inspiration to people who love their homes. You can shop from Pottery Barn by calling 1-800-922-5507, by visiting us online at www.potterybarn.com, or by stopping by a store near you.

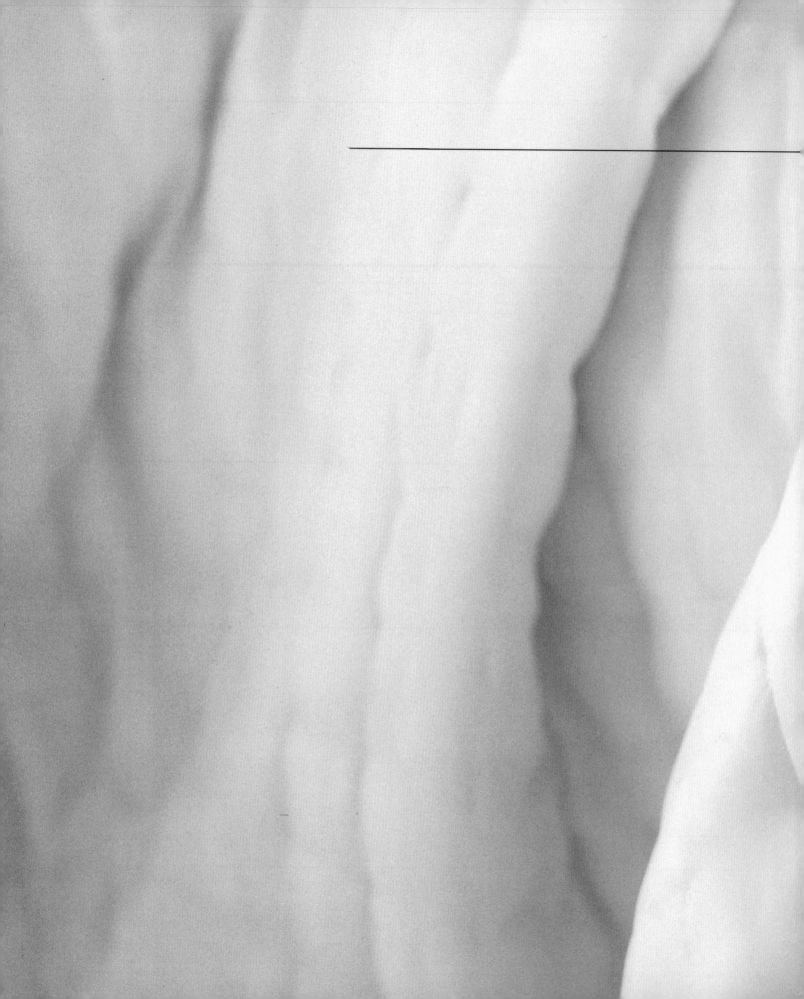